INFINITE HOPE

*in the midst of struggles*

# *infinite* HOPE
## IN THE MIDST OF STRUGGLES

Joni and Friends

Tyndale House Publishers, Inc.
Carol Stream, Illinois

LIVING
EXPRESSIONS
COLLECTION

*Living Expressions* invites you to explore God's Word
and express your creativity in ways that are refreshing
to the spirit and restorative to the soul.

Visit Tyndale online at www.tyndale.com.

Visit Joni and Friends online at www.joniandfriends.org.

TYNDALE, Tyndale's quill logo, *Living Expressions*, and the Living Expressions logo are registered trademarks
of Tyndale House Publishers, Inc.

The Joni and Friends logo is a trademark of Joni and Friends. *Beyond Suffering* is a registered trademark of Joni
and Friends.

*Infinite Hope . . . in the Midst of Struggles*

Designed by Mark Anthony Lane II

Published in association with the literary agency of The Denzel Agency, www.denzel.org.

For information about special discounts for bulk purchases, please contact Tyndale House Publishers at
csresponse@tyndale.com, or call 1-800-323-9400.

ISBN 978-1-4964-3223-0

Printed in China

24  23  22  21  20  19  18
 7   6   5   4   3   2   1

# contents

*foreword from Joni*

# Before You Begin . . .

Because you are holding this book in your hands, I believe it's safe to say you are interested in *hope*—understanding it, finding it, and resting in it. Our world is in terrible turmoil: People are angry, cynicism and despair are on the rise, and the nightly news reminds us we are only one terrorist plot away from another global nightmare. We desperately need soul-settling hope, the kind of hope that's infinite—never fading and always brightening our darkest paths. We need the hope of God to fill and overflow our hearts, transforming us into people who are confident and at peace with ourselves, our God, and our circumstances.

You may not realize it—and it may seem odd—but the sufferings scratching at your door are the very windows through which God wants to shine his brightest rays of hope. I should know. Suffering has been my constant companion ever since 1967, when I broke my neck in a diving accident and became a quadriplegic.

It was a terrible shock at first. When I learned that my paralysis was permanent, I sank into a deep depression. Then, after I returned from the hospital, my depression evolved into suicidal despair. I would often wrench my head back and forth on my pillow, hoping to break my neck at a higher vertebra, sever my spinal cord, and end my life. When that didn't work, I stayed in bed every morning for nearly two weeks, telling my sister, Kathy, to close the drapes, turn out the lights, and shut the door. Hope was nowhere to be found.

Lying there, I would brood over how much I hated being paralyzed. But I also hated the suffocation of self-pity. Slowly I realized I could not live with hopelessness. It was too claustrophobic, too confining. I finally cried out, "Oh, God, if I cannot die, then *please* show me how to live!" My prayer was short, but the God of all hope heard me.

The next morning, I woke up with a new determination to face life. I asked Kathy to get me up and into my wheelchair. Once I was in my chair, she pushed me into the living room and placed my Bible on a music stand in front of me. Clenching a mouth stick between my teeth, I began turning the pages. I knew the Bible contained answers for my plight; I just didn't know where to look.

Thankfully, God brought wise Christian friends alongside to help me discover his life-transforming precepts. I heard God whisper, *Joni, trust me . . . I have a bigger plan and more than enough power to change things. If I loved you enough to die for you, can't I be trusted with even this?* My hopelessness began to dissipate, especially when I read, "I pray that God, the source of hope, will fill you completely with joy and peace because you trust in him. Then you will overflow with confident hope through the power of the Holy Spirit" (Romans 15:13).

This was no ordinary hope that filled my heart. This was life-transforming hope—the kind that filled me with confidence and helped me find peace with myself, with God, and with my wheelchair. And I've never been the same since. Suffering was the wide-open window through which God shone his healing grace and infinite hope into my life. And it was my suffering that gave me a richer, deeper love for Christ, the Blessed Hope.

Perhaps you are caving in under the weight of suffering today—permanent pain from a botched surgery, an unexpected death in the family, or a divorce that totally took you by surprise. Perhaps your reputation has been unfairly stained, or your teenager has chosen a rebellious path toward drugs, or you are keeping vigil at the bedside of your little one who is struggling against cancer. It could simply be a long season of unexplained depression, the kind that lingers on and on like a low-grade fever. Do you wonder if you will ever smile again?

It is my prayer that the stories we share on the following pages, as well as the insights about suffering and the goodness of God, will fill your heart with this life-giving hope. May you gain a fresh perspective on your hardships and heartaches. I ask only that you read with prayerful expectancy of the hope and help God desires to shine upon you this day.

Infinite hope *is* possible. It's a little like the line from *The Shawshank Redemption* where Andy writes to his paroled friend, "Hope is a good thing, maybe the best of things. And no good thing ever dies."

I pray that with this special book as your guide, you will get busy living. And you can start right now by turning the page to find your much-needed inspiration and hope. Remember, hope is the *best* of things.

*Joni*

*Joni Eareckson Tada*

# *infinite*
# ASSURANCE

*Why am I discouraged?*
*Why is my heart so sad?*
*I will put my hope in God!*
*I will praise him again—*
*my Savior and my God!*

PSALM 42:11

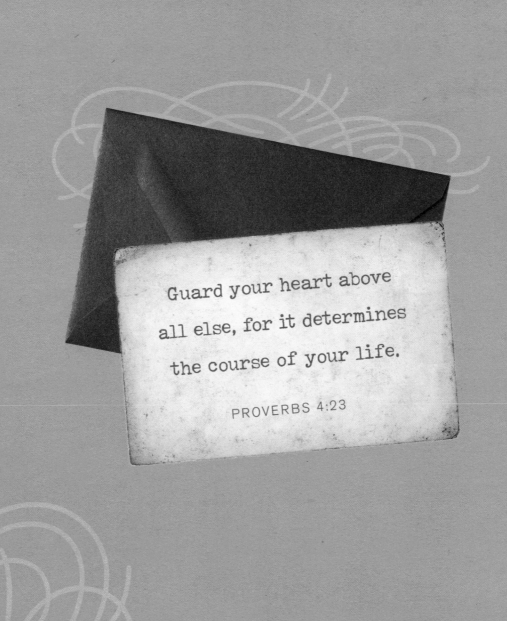

Guard your heart above all else, for it determines the course of your life.

PROVERBS 4:23

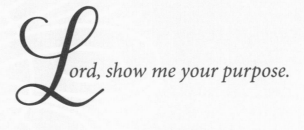

*L*ord, *show me your purpose.*

Life's struggles always prompt heart-wrenching questions:

> If God is good, why would he allow heartache and
>    pain in my life?
> Is God truly concerned about life-altering accidents,
>    natural disasters, and family crises, or does the
>    devil set the world's agenda?
> What is the purpose of this sadness in my life?

The psalmist David lamented,

*My God, my God, why have you abandoned me?*

  *Why are you so far away when I groan for help?*

*Every day I call to you, my God, but you do not answer.*

  *Every night I lift my voice, but I find no relief.*

PSALM 22:1-2

Does this sound familiar? Maybe you're walking a path of sorrows because of a job loss, a health issue, conflict with a loved one, a disability, or depression. Or perhaps you recall that David's first question was also spoken from the lips of a totally innocent man while he was hanging on a cruel cross (see Matthew 27:46). Jesus' expression of his profound sense of abandonment shows that he understands the spoken (and unspoken) questions in your life.

Jesus also put his humanity on full display in Gethsemane, telling his disciples, "My soul is crushed with grief to the point of death." Slipping further away, Jesus cries out, "Abba, Father, everything is possible for you. Please take this cup of suffering away from me." Then he models humanity attuned to divinity: "Yet I want your will to be done, not mine" (Mark 14:34-36).

It was excruciating for Jesus to place such suffering in God's hands, but he did. This Suffering Servant was described as "despised and rejected—a man of sorrows, acquainted with deepest grief" (Isaiah 53:3). Isaiah's prophecy foretold the crucifixion and burial of Jesus, who would bear our weaknesses and carry our sorrows. He would be pierced for our sins and rebellion, whipped and beaten for our healing. Our sins would be laid on him. His death would be undeserved—like a lamb being led to slaughter without resistance. His body would be buried in a rich man's grave. His death would (miraculously) produce a host of descendants, and he would be satisfied by the accomplishments of his anguish.

Jesus Christ shows us in a personal way what God looks like. Those who have become God's children by faith in Christ are daily being made more like him. The presence of personal crises, diseases, and struggles do nothing to negate this reality because all human beings bear the image of God and are capable of entering into a relationship with him (see Colossians 1:15, 2 Corinthians 3:18, and Genesis 1:26-27).

If your desire is to grapple with the meaning of adversity and learn to manage it, you must spend time in God's Word. Since Eden, people acquainted with suffering have looked to the character of God for justice, fresh purpose, and *infinite assurance* to carry on.

## When Hopelessness Crushes Your Spirit

At the age of twenty, Mike King had it all. He was a man's man: strong, athletic, and handsome. And then one day a car pulled out in front of the motorcycle Mike was riding, and *CRASH!*—his life was changed forever. Mike was left paralyzed, broken, and angry. He'd always been active in all kinds of sports and enjoyed meeting challenges head-on. But paralysis was a different story. Unable to walk, Mike struggled to find life's purpose.

When our hearts are sad and our spirits broken, we lose the strength to endure. Extended times of suffering take a toll that is magnified if we are not intentionally seeking God in their midst. Solomon cautions us, "Guard your heart above all else, for it determines the course of your life" (Proverbs 4:23). If we do not take precautions to protect and care for our hearts, it is to our own detriment.

SEARCH FOR THE LORD AND FOR HIS STRENGTH, CONTINUALLY SEEK HIM

1 CHRONICLES 16:11

How should we respond when we realize that we've forsaken our faith and left our hearts vulnerable to Satan's attack? The psalmist cried out,

*Create in me a clean heart, O God.*
   *Renew a loyal spirit within me. . . .*
*The sacrifice you desire is a broken spirit.*
   *You will not reject a broken and repentant heart, O God.*

PSALM 51:10, 17

During our darkest hours, when all comfort fails to touch the depth of our pain, Jesus stands with open arms as the ultimate expression of empathy and love—our model for suffering (see Isaiah 53:3-4). Like the psalmist, we can ask for God's merciful touch and rest assured that he will answer our prayers.

A few years after Mike King's accident, he heard about two wheelchair athletes who had traversed the continental United States in their chairs. The idea aroused his competitive nature and compelled him to do something even more daring—he set a wild goal to push his wheelchair from Fairbanks, Alaska, to Washington, DC.

Mike started out with his eye on the prize, but the long hours of wear on his hands and arms quickly brought discouragement. When some high school students heard about his goal, they showed support by surrounding him on their bikes. Others joined in along the way, and Mike completed the 5,605-mile trip, which changed his self-image and views on life.

The physical and spiritual discipline from Mike's earlier years helped transform him into a stalwart follower of Jesus Christ. Mike discovered new possibilities. Some years later, he founded an organization, Powered to Move, to promote physical fitness among persons with disabilities and to increase their physical, emotional, and spiritual well-being. Today, he and his wife, Sharyn, travel around the world sharing the hope of Jesus Christ with hurting people.

People ask Mike what keeps him connected to God in the daily grind of a disability. With a winning smile, he says, "It is the hope Christ provides. God has a plan for each of us. It's not a plan B—it's a plan A, and it doesn't change. He has shown me this throughout my experiences and led me right to where I am today."

No matter what we are facing, the Lord assures us that he is aware of our circumstances and present with us:

> *For I know the plans I have for you. . . . They are*
> *plans for good and not for disaster, to give you a*
> *future and a hope.*
> JEREMIAH 29:11

> *My thoughts are nothing like your thoughts. . . .*
> *And my ways are far beyond anything you could*
> *imagine.*
> ISAIAH 55:8

*a word from Joni*

# I Need God in My Suffering

When we wonder why we must suffer, we're actually asking a question of someone. That someone is God. But why he allowed suffering doesn't really matter. The only thing that matters is how we respond. When we can't find the answer we're looking for, we can find peace in the only true answer: We need God!

Affliction is the lowest common denominator for all of us. Philippians 1:29 tells us to expect suffering: "For you have been given not only the privilege of trusting in Christ but also the privilege of suffering for him." But no matter how strong our faith is, it's natural to ask why.

After many years of suffering, I've concluded that God allows one form of evil—suffering—to expose another form of evil—sin. It is as if God were turning suffering on its head to help us feel the sting of sin, which reminds us of how poisonous sin really is. Suffering is like a sandblaster that strips away our fears, anxieties, self-centeredness, complaining, and apathy toward others who hurt. God allows affliction to rip it all away so that we can see the world through the eyes of Christ.

God hates evil and suffering. He promises us in his Word that he will relieve suffering, and he relieves it every day. We can be sure that if our hearts hurt for someone, God felt our pain first. Our souls are strengthened through suffering. To know God better, we must know our suffering better. And as we do, we become less self-focused and more God-focused.

Lord, you're the Creator of the universe and everything in it—nothing is hidden from you. You see doubts and hurts; you're acquainted with my grief. But none of it makes any sense to me. I need to understand your infinite purpose for these things . . .

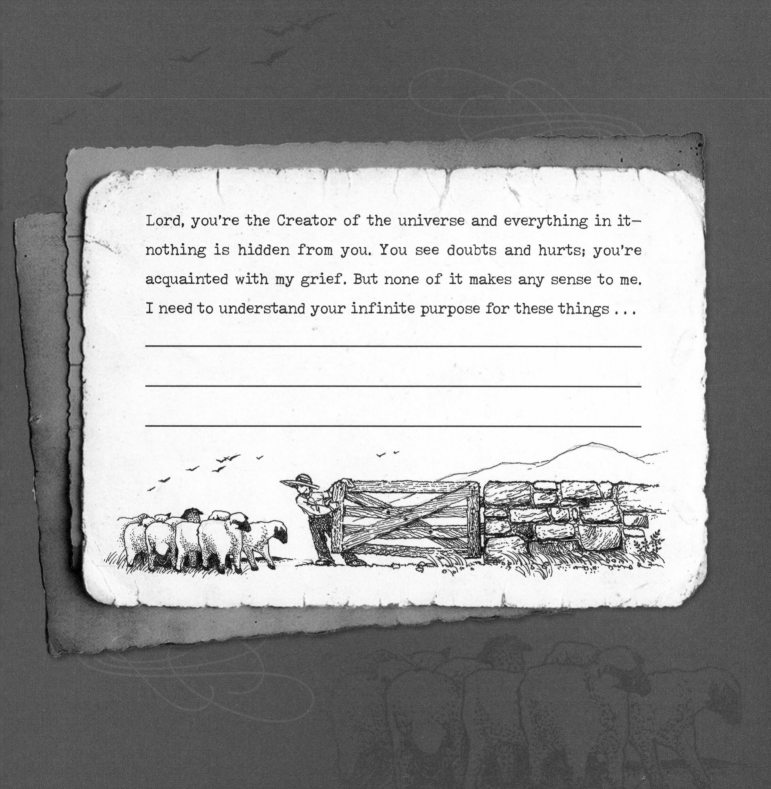

## *You Are God's Masterpiece*

We are made in God's own image—something unique to humanity (see Genesis 1:26-27). While our capacity to reflect the divine image is impacted by sin, the image itself remains intact. Thus all human beings, whatever their abilities or struggles, are "image bearers" and capable of having a relationship with God. We share the common dignity and equal value that being made in God's image confers.

This is true whether we "feel" like it or not. Yet at some point, we all try to hide from ourselves and from others, pulling the covers over our heads so God doesn't even have to look at us. These emotions can be the result of sin in our lives, but often they come from the constant trouble and stress that weigh us down. Life on this earth is incomplete and even contradictory at times. We rarely have all the explanations we desire for the conflicting circumstances of life, especially when we feel painfully alone.

Even John the Baptist, who had a pretty clear idea about who Jesus was and about his own purpose in life, experienced serious doubts when he found himself in prison. He sent some of his followers to ask Jesus, "Are you the Messiah we've been expecting, or should we keep looking for someone else?" (Matthew 11:3). Somehow, suffering in prison didn't align with John's expectations if Jesus was in fact the Messiah John thought he was.

We, too, can begin to doubt God when our lives don't make sense or our expectations are not met. We wonder whether God is who we thought he was when we first met him. But God's plans are not subject to our desires or dreams. His purposes for us often involve suffering and pain in this present world.

Jesus' reply to John's disciples was gentle and understanding—yet also challenging: "Go back to John and tell him what you have heard and seen" (Matthew 11:4). And Jesus added, "God blesses those who do not fall away because of me" (verse 6).

FOR WE ARE GOD'S MASTERPIECE. HE HAS CREATED US ANEW IN CHRIST JESUS.

EPHESIANS 2:10

Such assurance inspired John to continue declaring the coming of the Messiah and calling many to repentance. He met his death at the hands of a vengeful woman and a weak king when Herodias, King Herod's wife, persuaded her daughter to ask Herod for John's head on a tray (see Matthew 14:1-12). To John's followers, it seemed that evil had won out, but Jesus honored him, saying that he was more than a prophet—he was God's messenger, faithful to his life's purpose (see Matthew 11:10-19).

In Ephesians, the apostle Paul sets the foundation for every believer. Our purpose is to praise and glorify God: "When you believed in Christ, he identified you as his own. . . . He has purchased us to be his own people. He did this so we would praise and glorify him" (Ephesians 1:13-14). Whatever our circumstances, sufferings, or disabilities, we fulfill our ultimate purpose and live out God's plans for us as we seek to glorify him.

# You Were Made for This

Ever wonder exactly why God created you? Or why he placed specific children in your family? God couldn't have spelled it out any plainer than in Isaiah 43:6-7:

> *I will say to the north and south,*
>     *"Bring my sons and daughters back to Israel*
>         *from the distant corners of the earth.*
> *Bring all who claim me as their God,*
>     *for I have made them for my glory.*
>     *It was I who created them."*

He created you and me for one purpose: to showcase his glory; to enjoy it, display it, and demonstrate it every day to all whom we encounter.

What does it mean to put God's glory on display? It means highlighting his attributes and characteristics. It means making hard choices to do the right thing. It means biting your tongue to keep from gossiping, going out of your way for a neighbor in need, telling the truth even when it's hard, not snapping back when someone hurts you, and speaking openly about your Father in heaven. In short, it's living as Jesus lived when he walked on earth.

God is invisible. In the Old Testament, his power and glory are displayed through visible things, such as the burning bush that was not consumed and the pillar of cloud and fire that led the Israelites through the desert. In the New Testament, God's glory is displayed through his Son, Jesus. But Jesus no longer physically walks on earth, and bushes *do* burn in prairie fires and in piles of raked foilage set aflame. So how does an invisible God display his glory in this age? Through you and your children. What a privilege!

*Father God, what an honor we've been given! You no longer choose to speak through inanimate objects; you choose people like us to show yourself to the world. Point out ways we can showcase your glorious qualities to others today. In so doing, we'll glorify you and live the life we were created for. Amen.*

## Increasing Assurance

Have you ever watched a baby when he is learning to walk? It can be an anxious experience filled with ups and downs. But there's no mistaking the determination (and often frustration) in his eyes as his little fingers grasp a chair and he struggles to pull himself to his feet. On shaky legs, he takes one step, then two; but because he's unwilling to let go of the chair, he eventually falls onto his diapered bottom in tearful protest. Then the process starts all over again.

Adults are often like babies learning to walk. We believe that God wants to strengthen our faith and use us in his service, but we don't want to exercise our spiritual muscles by facing emotional and physical hardships. We prefer to see the whole picture before letting go of our sense of security. Yet over time, suffering has a way of moving us forward to a more mature walk with the Lord.

## THE CHRISTIAN LIFE

Assurance grows by repeated conflict, by our repeated experimental proof of the Lord's power and goodness to save; when we have been brought very low and helped, sorely wounded and healed, cast down and raised again; have given up all hope and been suddenly snatched from danger and placed in safety; and when these things have been repeated to us and in us a thousand times over, we begin to learn to trust simply to the word and power of God, beyond and against appearances: and this trust, when habitual and strong, bears the name of assurance; for even assurance has degrees.

JOHN NEWTON (1724–1807)

The apostle Paul wrote, "I am glad when I suffer for you in my body, for I am participating in the sufferings of Christ that continue for his body, the church" (Colossians 1:24). But consider Paul's journey to this life of surrender. After his head-on collision with Jesus Christ on the way to Damascus (see Acts 9:1-6), he miraculously stopped persecuting believers and became a great missionary to the Gentiles. His life of suffering for the sake of the gospel included imprisonment and beatings with whips and rods. He was stoned and shipwrecked and faced danger in cities and deserts and on the sea. He suffered many burdens, weaknesses, and periods of running from enemies set to destroy him (see 2 Corinthians 11:16-30). Through all this, Paul's consistent life of faith and expectancy of our Lord's return enabled him to become the most prolific writer in the New Testament. While we can't all be "Pauls," we can passionately seek God's purpose and strive to accomplish it in our own lives.

Apart from God, suffering is meaningless, but in his hands it brings others to faith in Jesus Christ. God has a way of using suffering for his glory and purposes. When we surrender ourselves—especially our weaknesses—to God, he completes those things we lack, making our lives "a Christ-like fragrance rising up to God" (2 Corinthians 2:15).

Our culture frowns upon acknowledging weakness. Although we are inspired by stories of others overcoming obstacles, we grow uncomfortable when tribulations hit close to home. We fear that admitting our struggles with mental illness, cancer, disability, or addiction may make us seem less capable. Many people suffer alone in fear of losing their jobs or friends—even church friends. No wonder we lose hope. But God's Word challenges us to rejoice in our weaknesses. Why? Because God assures us that when we are weak, we are also strong. He reveals this mystery to the believers in Corinth: "My grace is all you need. My power works best in weakness" (2 Corinthians 12:9).

What are you holding on to that keeps you from confidently embracing God's purpose for your life? Write a prayer releasing it to God and thanking him for his promise of assurance.

_____

_____

_____

## The Path of Endurance

Missionary and professor Larry Waters has suffered with debilitating cluster headaches for more than eighteen years. They are so severe that he often refers to them as "suicide headaches." His wife, Mary, is usually awakened in the night when Larry falls to the floor, crying out to God and begging him to stop the pain. Mary quickly tries to help by placing his head in her lap and holding ice packs on Larry's face. She helps with his medication and waits with him for it to take effect. Mary speaks softly, and her touch means so much. Larry sees the worry and concern in her eyes. He knows that she would do anything to make his pain stop.

Mary doesn't have to wonder what Job's wife felt as she saw her boil-ridden, suffering husband sitting among the ashes, feeling helpless. Unlike Job's wife, who suggested that death might be better than a miserable life (see Job 2:9), Mary has always tried to be an encourager, and she prays fervently for Larry's pain to stop. She rejoices with him during periods of relief and peace. "We can cherish the life God has given us," says Mary, "even in the face of excruciating suffering."

We all hate to suffer and see our loved ones in ongoing pain. News reports about laws establishing one's "right to die" urge society to accept euthanasia as common practice and even make the argument that it is a kind and merciful approach. But the book of Job makes it clear that suicide and euthanasia reflect godless thinking and are unacceptable ways of dealing with suffering and disability. We must choose the path of endurance in the life God has given us. Larry and Mary Waters make that choice daily, honoring the Lord by the way they live.

> *God might kill me, but I have no other hope.*
>    *I am going to argue my case with him.*
>
> JOB 13:15

## One Woman's Brave Voice

You may not know Fanny Crosby's name, but if you grew up in church, you've probably sung one of the eight thousand hymns or gospel songs she penned during her lifetime. Fanny was an inspiration to many, and for much more than just her prolific writing. Blind because of an illness shortly after birth, she lived out her days during the nineteenth century, when people with disabilities had few rights and were viewed by many as unable to be educated.

Thankfully, her family encouraged her love of writing, music, and memorizing Scripture. They enrolled her at the New York Institution for the Blind, where she graduated and later returned as an instructor. Fanny also became an advocate for the blind, lobbying in support of their education. During this time, she gained recognition as a poet and met President James K. Polk, Henry Clay, and William Cullen Bryant. She also recited some of her poetry before senators and representatives in Congress Assembly Hall. The audience included Jefferson Davis and former president John Quincy Adams. She was also the first woman to speak to the Senate.

While Fanny was a brave voice for those with disabilities and for the poor and needy, she also experienced many hardships. Her only child, a daughter, died in her sleep when only a few months old. With a mom's grieving heart, Fanny wrote the hymn "Safe in the Arms of Jesus." She always found solace in the psalms, especially those that encouraged her to hold on until the day she would see her Savior's face. Other beloved songs Fanny wrote include "He Hideth My Soul" and "To God Be the Glory." Her songs and poems continue to bring comfort and hope to people throughout the world.

# Blessed Assurance

LYRICS BY FANNY J. CROSBY, 1820–1915
MUSIC BY PHOEBE PALMER KNAPP, 1839–1908

Blessed assurance, Jesus is mine!
O what a foretaste of glory divine!
Heir of salvation, purchase of God,
Born of His Spirit, washed in His blood.

*(Refrain)*
This is my story, this is my song,
Praising my Savior all the day long;
This is my story, this is my song,
Praising my Savior all the day long.

Perfect submission, perfect delight!
Visions of rapture now burst on my sight;
Angels descending bring from above
Echoes of mercy, whispers of love.

Perfect submission—all is at rest,
I in my Savior am happy and blest;
Watching and waiting, looking above,
Filled with His goodness, lost in His love.

REJOICE *in our* CONFIDENT HOPE. BE PATIENT IN TROUBLE & KEEP on PRAYING.

ROMANS 12 : 12

## You Can Be Joyful

Inevitably, trouble will come into the lives of God's people. Few things sap one's energy, joy, and enthusiasm quicker than nagging doubt, chronic pain, and isolation. These kinds of things are tools the enemy uses to steal our joy. But we can defeat the enemy by believing that God is always present and knows what we are going through. He has a plan in place to help us. That's why the apostle Paul encourages us to "Rejoice in our confident hope. Be patient in trouble, and keep on praying" (Romans 12:12).

Fanny Crosby may have been tempted in the midst of her blindness to wallow in depression, but her hymns ring true to the unchangeable character of God, who is "the same yesterday, today, and forever" (Hebrews 13:8). He is always ready to hear our prayers, give us patience, and restore our confidence—no matter how often we need his reassurance.

Consider Pat Verbal's story. In ten short years, her beloved husband, Stan, went from being a busy aerospace engineer and an avid fisherman to a man totally dependent on full-time care. Yet he never lost his gentleness and warm smile that radiated from his deep faith in a loving God.

"The hardest part of living with a loved one with Alzheimer's is the constant change," says Pat. "I never knew what to expect next. Sometimes change came slowly, and other times it felt like I was watching meticulous rows of dominos tumbling downhill."

In the early years, Pat saw the disease as something happening to her sweet husband who needed her help. But as Stan moved into mid- and late-stage memory loss, God made it clear that the crisis was also happening to her.

"I discovered that we were on this journey together, and that God intended it for my own growth in grace and character. I began to focus on the changes inside my own heart, and that made all the difference. We were able to celebrate each day as a gift from God, and I could sing over my high school sweetheart as I released him into the arms of our Savior."

*I, the LORD, made you,*
   *and I will not forget you.*
ISAIAH 44:21

*Don't be afraid, for I am with you.*
   *Don't be discouraged, for I am your God.*
*I will strengthen you and help you.*
   *I will hold you up with my victorious right hand.*
ISAIAH 41:10

People often tell Joni Eareckson Tada how attractive she is—that her smile is warm and inviting. She is usually quick to remind them that her joy comes from within. Like many who suffer with an ongoing disability, each new day is a challenge. Here is how Joni describes it:

On an average day, Ken leaves for work and a friend comes to get me up. While she makes coffee, I usually pray, "Lord, my friend is about to give me a bath, get me dressed, sit me up in my chair, brush my hair and teeth, and send me out the door. I don't have the strength to face this routine one more time. I have no resources. I don't have a smile for the day, but you do. May I borrow yours? I urgently need you, God."

So when my friend walks into the bedroom, I turn my head on my pillow and give her a smile sent straight from heaven. It's not my own smile—it's God's. "Whatever joy you see today"—I tell her as I gesture at my paralyzed legs—"was hard-won this morning." I have learned that the weaker we are, the harder we must lean on God. And the harder we lean on him, the stronger we discover him to be.

He that believes on me,
out of him shall flow
rivers of living water.

John 7:38

Lord, I choose to rejoice in my growing confidence
in your plan for me. I will be patient and keep
praying over all my struggles. I'm ready to stretch
my spiritual muscles as I trust you with . . .

_____

_____

_____

Are you feeling weak today? When your joy and courage come from God's strength, people can't help but notice the infinite hope you possess. Just make sure they know where it came from!

Assurance is a fruit
that grows out of
the root of faith.

STEPHEN CHARNOCK

# PART 2

# *infinite*
# POSSIBILITIES

*Dear brothers and sisters, when troubles of any kind come
your way, consider it an opportunity for great joy.
For you know that when your faith is tested,
your endurance has a chance to grow.*

JAMES 1:2-3

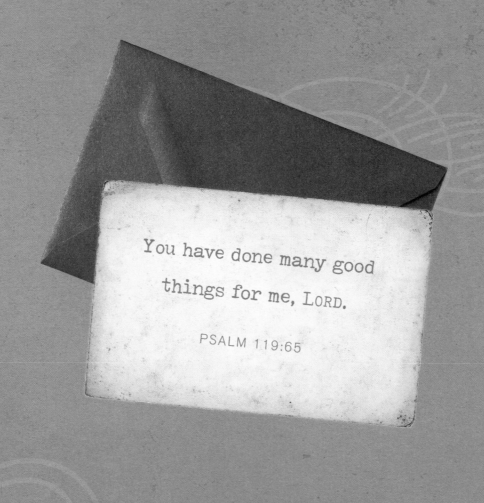

You have done many good things for me, LORD.

PSALM 119:65

*Lord, grant me faith in times of trouble.*

Sometimes it seems there is nothing left to say except . . . *Help, Lord!*

You're trying to solve a troubling problem head-on. You scrutinize the issue, jot down action plans, and talk to those involved, but the situation gets worse. You seek wise counsel, pray through sleepless nights, and consult Scripture, which instructs you to be patient and long-suffering. Yet time passes, and the unpaid bills mount, the medication doesn't help, the weariness continues, and the hurt doesn't heal. The growing stress pushes all your old buttons, tempting you to return to sinful patterns that could wreck your witness—maybe your life.

What does one do when faced with life's impossibilities?

While you may feel isolated, it's crucial to remember that even in our darkest days, we are not alone. The same God who parted the Red Sea for the Israelites, held the sun in place for Joshua, provided a sacrifice for Abraham, and gave up his only Son is with us. He encourages us, "Do not be afraid or discouraged. For the LORD your God is with you wherever you go" (Joshua 1:9). He takes notice of and cares about every struggle, pain, and loss that you experience. You don't have to fear troubles, because you matter to God. He loves you more than you can imagine and promises to be with you in good times and bad. God may not move according to our timetables—it may take years before his infinite possibilities are revealed to us. That's why *faith* makes all the difference. The possibilities are boundless once we decide to act in faith and not simply react to our struggles.

Poet William Blake wrote, "If the doors of perception were cleansed every thing would appear to man as it is, Infinite."

## Your Antidote for Unanswered Prayer

Every culture in the ancient Near East saw infertility as a curse. In the book of 1 Samuel, that was Hannah's situation—her barrenness brought her great shame and grief, especially when her husband's other wife had several children. Although her husband, Elkanah, loved her, Hannah's emptiness took its toll, reducing her to tears many times. In her desperation, Hannah poured out her pain before the Lord during an annual pilgrimage to the Tabernacle and bargained with him for a child (see 1 Samuel 1:1-18).

Often, our pain resonates so deep that only the Lord is able to fully understand it. In those moments, we can rest assured that there is no limit to how far his caring touch extends. The antidote to discouragement in times of trouble is to pour out our hearts before the Lord. It's the process of laying down our burdens at his feet that makes it possible for us to receive his blessing and ultimately to move from discouragement to refreshment. Consider these passages from the book of Psalms:

> *Trust in [the Lord] at all times.*
> *Pour out your heart to him,*
> *for God is our refuge.*
>
> PSALM 62:8

> *I will call to [the Lord] whenever*
> *I'm in trouble,*
> *and you will answer me.*
>
> PSALM 86:7

> *In times of trouble, may the LORD answer your cry.*
> *May the name of the God of Jacob keep you safe*
> *from all harm. . . .*
> *May he grant your heart's desires*
> *and make all your plans succeed.*
>
> PSALM 20:1, 4

Hannah is an example for all who wrestle with unrealized dreams. In God's perfect timing, she gave birth to her son, Samuel. After he was weaned, she faithfully relinquished him to serve in the Tabernacle as she had promised. Her sacrificial act required tremendous faith in God, which she expressed in a prayer of praise:

> *My heart rejoices in the LORD!*
> *The LORD has made me strong.*
> *Now I have an answer for my enemies;*
> *I rejoice because you rescued me.*

1 SAMUEL 2:1

## Trusting God in the Meantime

"Trouble" could have been Joseph's middle name. In every family, there seems to be one person who is constantly standing under a storm cloud, dripping wet, being pounded by lightning and thunder. To say Joseph couldn't catch a break would be a gross understatement.

Joseph knew the pain of being betrayed by his own flesh and blood—his brothers, who had rejected and nearly killed him, opted instead to sell him into a life of slavery (see Genesis 37:18-36). As a servant to Potiphar in Egypt, Joseph tasted the bitter pill of injustice when Potiphar's wife falsely accused him of assaulting her, landing him in prison without due process and with no release in sight (see Genesis 39:6-20). Sitting alone in a dungeon for at least two years, Joseph knew the nausea of hunger, the stench of decay, the insanity of isolation. Such anguish would tempt even the strongest person to become bitter and hateful, to abandon all hope. But the Lord was with him (see Genesis 39:21) and Joseph remained faithful, even though he had no way of knowing that God would use him to save an entire nation from famine and starvation. He couldn't have known that his family would eventually be reunited. He couldn't have envisioned that he would someday be second in command to Pharaoh himself, wielding immense power in a land neither of his birth nor of his choosing. God had not forgotten Joseph. Ultimately, God saved many lives through him (see Genesis 45:7).

Have you had a dungeon-like experience where you've felt abandoned? Have you cried out to God, wondering whether he even hears? Take heart: God has not forgotten you.

The LORD
IS MY LIGHT &
MY SALVATION
SO WHY SHOULD
I be
AFRAID?

PSALM 27:1

Lord, in the midst of trouble, I want to humble myself in your sight. I believe you will be faithful to lift me up—in your time, for your purpose, and for your glory.

_____

_____

_____

_____

_____

## *Your Lifeline in Times of Despair*

When tragedy strikes, we fear that we may never again have a reason to rejoice. But no matter how hard the circumstances or how severe the suffering, God is in the business of redeeming our pain. The book of Ruth teaches us that when we feel as if we are drowning in a black sea of impossibilities, our Redeemer stands by with a secure lifeline.

When Israel's rich land of plenty was ravaged by famine, an Israelite named Elimelech did what he thought was best, moving his family to Moab. Then he died, leaving his wife, Naomi, to raise their two sons alone. The boys grew up and married Moabite women, and life went on—until both of her sons died, and Naomi again felt the devastating sting of death. Everyone and everything she had held dear was gone, and she faced the ultimate challenge: Would she abandon all hope and give up? Or could she continue to follow God and trust him with her future?

People today are often confronted with similar circumstances. Modern technology enables us to watch as lives are destroyed by floods, fires, wars, hurricanes, and earthquakes. Whether it's the loss of a dream or the death of a loved one, there are times of unimaginable hardship in life.

In the midst of unspeakable loss, Naomi remained faithful to God. When she learned the famine was over, she decided to return to her homeland of Bethlehem. Both of her daughters-in-law started the journey with her, but along the way, Naomi urged them to go back to their familiar homeland. Yet one of them—Ruth—chose to turn her back on the false gods of her youth and follow Naomi to an unknown land. They set out for "home" with a fresh devotion to one another and to God. Despite their grief, they continued to move forward.

As Naomi reunited with her kinfolk, she confessed her deep bitterness. But God's goodness proved to be more powerful than the bitterness Naomi felt over her losses. God not only provided for Naomi and Ruth's daily needs but also gave Ruth a new husband named Boaz—a powerful picture of redemption and grace. In a society in which widows were especially vulnerable, Boaz provided protection and a secure future for both women. Moreover, he and Ruth were blessed with a son, Obed, through whom this humble family became part of the genealogical history of Jesus Christ himself (see Ruth 1–4).

If your heart is weighed down with sorrow and you're standing at a crossroads, there is a place for you in the Father's house (see John 14:2). There you'll discover, as Naomi and Ruth did, both deliverance from devastating grief in the here and now and pleasures in God's presence in heaven forevermore.

Despair, temptation, grief, and other symptoms of suffering can bring out the worst and the best in us. Throughout the Gospels, Jesus' approach was countercultural, establishing a new model for his followers to emulate. In the book of Matthew, Jesus provides a framework—also known as the Beatitudes—for how believers ought to live, especially in the face of persecution and evil:

> *God blesses those who are poor and realize their need for him,*
>     *for the Kingdom of Heaven is theirs.*
> *God blesses those who mourn,*
>     *for they will be comforted.*
> *God blesses those who are humble,*
>     *for they will inherit the whole earth.*
> *God blesses those who hunger and thirst for justice,*
>     *for they will be satisfied.*
> *God blesses those who are merciful,*
>     *for they will be shown mercy.*

*God blesses those whose hearts are pure,*

*for they will see God.*

*God blesses those who work for peace,*

*for they will be called the children of God.*

*God blesses those who are persecuted for doing right,*

*for the Kingdom of Heaven is theirs.*

MATTHEW 5:3-10

And just about the time we are convinced we can never measure up, Paul assures us we can "do everything through Christ, who gives [us] strength" (Philippians 4:13).

FOR I CAN DO EVERYTHING THROUGH CHRIST, WHO GIVES ME STRENGTH.

PHILIPPIANS 4:13

## *You Can Be God's Light*

We serve a God of possibilities. He wants hearts that are burning with passion for future things, on fire for Kingdom realities that are out of this world. God wants his people to be aflame with his hope and to have an outlook of pure joy that affects how they live. God wants each of us to be "like a city on a hilltop" (Matthew 5:14) and "a lamp . . . placed on a stand" (Matthew 5:15) so that everyone around us will be encouraged to look heavenward.

A perspective like this isn't gained without suffering. Affliction fuels the furnace of heaven-hearted hope. People whose lives are unscathed by affliction have a less energetic hope. Oh, they are glad to know they are going to heaven; for them, accepting Jesus is a guaranteed agreement for the future. Once it's taken care of, they feel they can get back to life as usual—dating and marrying, working and vacationing, saving and spending.

But suffering obliterates such earthly preoccupations. Suffering wakes us up from our spiritual slumber and turns our hearts toward the future, like a mother turning the face of her child, insisting, "Look this way!"

When Katie was born with a neurobiological disorder, doctors said she would be intellectually disabled. This crushing news hit her parents hard. But one day this toddler looked out the car window and read a street sign. Katie's parents gave her a book, which she also read. They soon discovered that Katie was hyperlexic. One unique aspect of that disorder is an exceptional, untaught ability to read words from a young age. As a fourth grader, Katie taught herself Japanese. She continued to strengthen her parents' faith and amaze her family with God's perfect plan for her life.

What has suffering taken from you? Don't allow your heart to dwell on such earthly disappointments. God permits suffering in order to draw our attention to heaven, where that which was lost—and more—shall be restored. Suffering forces us to look forward to the limitless possibilities God has for us now and in eternity. Until then, we have work to do! Jesus says, "We must quickly carry out the tasks assigned us by the one who sent us. The night is coming, and then no one can work" (John 9:4).

What has God assigned to you? How does Christ's light shine through you?

## A Path to the Light

Howard was a successful businessman, a husband, and a devoted father. In his midforties, he was paralyzed in a car accident. After the accident, he determined to recover quickly and not see himself as a victim. Howard's positive, upbeat attitude impressed everyone. Soon he was back at work, maneuvering his wheelchair through airports on business trips, not letting anything stand in his way. But Howard had a secret: He was struggling with increasing anxiety. A severe panic attack ultimately sent him to the hospital and into therapy.

Howard's determination to overcome the life-changing accident caused him to deny his crushed spirit and his grief. These unexpressed emotions created anxiety that became too great to control. Ironically, Howard's "positive attitude" ended up hurting him. His outer self took the significant life change in stride, but his inner self was in deep pain.

Through therapy, Howard learned to acknowledge his feelings, especially the painful ones. He learned that his anxiety was a signal he needed to pay attention to and that it was important not to deny his feelings. Physical pain can be a gift from God to warn us that our bodies are being harmed. Similarly, our emotions can be God-given indicators that something is wrong and needs to be addressed.

Expressing and acknowledging our emotions in a healthy way can also help us to connect with God and others. As the apostle Paul said, "He comforts us in all our troubles so that we can comfort others. When they are troubled, we will be able to give them the same comfort God has given us" (2 Corinthians 1:4). We live in a world with emotional and physical suffering, but we do not have to go through it alone.

Like Howard, the apostle Paul discovered that his weakness was part of his strength.

*I was given a thorn in my flesh, a messenger from Satan to torment me and keep me from becoming proud.*

*Three different times I begged the Lord to take it away. Each time he said, "My grace is all you need. My power works best in weakness." So now I am glad to boast about my weaknesses, so that the power of Christ can work through me.*

2 CORINTHIANS 12:7-9

This is how Paul came to see God's possibilities throughout the many insults, hardships, persecutions, and troubles that he suffered. God's strength always works best in our weaknesses, keeping us from taking pride in our own accomplishments. Our personal struggles serve as constant reminders not only of our weaknesses but also of Christ's sufficient grace and power to light the world through us.

HE GIVES POWER to the WEAK · AND STRENGTH to the POWERLESS·

ISAIAH 40:29

Lord of infinite possibilities, I turn my heart toward you today. I set my mind and emotions on you and relinquish all my efforts to "fix" my circumstances on my own. You are the Light of the world. Show me how to shine!

_____

_____

_____

_____

47

# My Faith Looks Up to Thee

LYRICS BY RAY PALMER, 1808–1887

MUSIC BY LOWELL MASON, 1792–1872

My faith looks up to Thee,
Thou Lamb of Calvary,
Savior divine!
Now hear me while I pray,
Take all my guilt away,
O let me from this day
Be wholly Thine!

May Thy rich grace impart
Strength to my fainting heart,
My zeal inspire;
As Thou hast died for me,
O may my love to Thee
Pure, warm, and changeless be,
A living fire!

While life's dark maze I tread
And griefs around me spread,
Be Thou my guide;
Bid darkness turn to day,
Wipe sorrow's tears away,
Nor let me ever stray
From Thee aside.

When ends life's passing dream,
When death's cold, threatening stream
Shall o'er me roll,
Blest Savior, then, in love,
Fear and distrust remove;
O lift me safe above,
A ransomed soul!

# Just Look Up

I love hymns, especially ones that talk about Jesus being near us, leading us, and strengthening our fainting hearts. But I'll be the first to confess that sometimes the Lord leads me down paths that seem to stray from his presence. These can lead to some very, very dark places, such as when God has made me lie in bed for weeks with pressure sores.

It's not a place I want to go, but after a few days of lying flat on my back, I start thinking, *Hey, God has led me here, and if I'm down on my back, the only thing I can do is look up!* I have to look up when I'm in bed; it's the only physical position I can lie in.

And when I look up at the ceiling, I remind myself of every encouraging Scripture I've memorized—such as Psalm 119:65: "You have done many good things for me, LORD." I need to remember that! Verse 71 says, "My suffering was good for me, for it taught me to pay attention to your decrees." And verse 50 states, "Your promise revives me; it comforts me in all my troubles."

God will never leave us—he will fulfill his purpose for us and carry his work in us on to completion (see Philippians 1:6). He'll pour out grace. He'll import hope. At times, he may lead us into some very dark places where we do not want to go. Not long after my injury, as I wrestled with uncertainty, I sketched a charcoal self-portrait capturing my fear and anguish; yet my eyes are turned toward heaven. Even in our darkest times, God is waiting for us to just look up.

## Giving Thanks for Everything

It's easy to be focused on God's will when things are going smoothly. It's quite different when we face failures, illnesses, or trials. First Thessalonians 5:18-19 says, "Be thankful in all circumstances, for this is God's will for you who belong to Christ Jesus. Do not stifle the Holy Spirit." We must understand that God is working out his purpose in each of our lives, and that purpose often includes suffering. We can thank him even in the worst of times because we believe that God has specifically designed our unique paths and that nothing comes into our lives that has not been filtered through his hands and redeemed through Christ's suffering.

Do not disdain the small. The whole of the life—even the hard—is made up of the minute parts, and if I miss the infinitesimals, I miss the whole. . . . There is a way to live the big of giving thanks in all things. It is this: to give thanks in this one small thing. The moments will add up.[1]

ANN VOSKAMP

## The Possibility That Christ Is Enough

At 7:50 a.m. on April 17, 2010, Megan Moss was semiconscious, lying in an intensive care unit with heart failure and pneumonia, surviving by means of a temporary respirator. Doctors told her parents that their twenty-three-year-old daughter was too ill to undergo a heart transplant, even if a donor became available. They concluded with these dreaded words: "There is nothing else we can do."

Megan's dad replied, "There is something we can do. We can pray." And pray they did: The global body of Christ who'd heard about Megan's condition on social media, in print and television news reports, and through local prayer chains went to their knees in earnest prayer. Her family took numerous walks around Megan's hospital bed, claiming victory in Jesus' name.

At 3:00 p.m., Megan underwent an emergency treatment for her severe infection and congestion. Several hours later, her temperature came down, her breathing eased, and for the first time in days, she asked for food. The cardiologist walked into Megan's room at 9:30 p.m. with a big grin and said, "Megan, we have a heart for you, if you choose to accept it!" She nodded yes. Megan's heart transplant was a miraculous success.

As she continued to get stronger, Megan felt the Lord leading her to start a blog where she could share her ongoing journey and express her deep faith in God. She also articulated a deep sense of grief and gratitude for the organ donor's family, whose dear loved one had given her a second chance to live a full life. Her motto was "Through this I demonstrate that Christ IS enough. Come what may."

Megan's glowing two-year-posttransplant checkup results indicated that her body was thriving with the new heart. It was not a surprise to her family and friends who had trusted God's plan in saving Megan's life for his purposes. Part of that divine plan included a young man named Nathan Johnson, her cousin's best friend, whom Megan had met several months after her heart surgery. Nathan and his parents had prayed for Megan the entire time she was hospitalized. Little did Nathan's parents know that the brave young woman they'd been praying for in April 2010 would become their daughter-in-law in October 2011.

After buying their first home in Nashville, Nathan and Megan were soon decorating a nursery for their first child. After a smooth delivery, Megan held Eilee Kate in her arms, feeding and burping her. It was a celebration for the entire family, but sadly, a short-lived one. Eight hours later, this thirty-one-year-old mother died of unforeseen complications. Words fail to describe the feelings Nathan experienced—as a new father, his overwhelming love for his baby girl was mixed with devastating grief at the loss of his beautiful wife and best friend. Nathan told friends that though his sadness and grief were very deep, he also felt hope as he held his daughter in his arms.

Megan was an enthusiastic supporter of organ donation, since she herself had received a heart transplant. After her death, Megan's organs were used to help more than fifty people, whose lives will forever be different because of Megan. Friends set up a GoFundMe page to raise support for Nathan and baby Eilee, and donations exceeded eight times the amount of their initial goal.[2]

"Our seven-month-old granddaughter, Eilee Kate, continues to deeply touch all those who love and care for her," say Megan's parents, Wayne and Kathie Moss. "This precious child is an ongoing testimony of the faith and hope Megan brought to her family and friends every day of her life. Her courageous story continues to change lives around the world."

In the Gospels, Christ healed people who had great faith and those who had little or no faith. But regardless of how much faith a person did or didn't have, Jesus did not choose to heal everyone. Sometimes God is glorified through a miraculous healing in our lives (see John 9:1-7). Other times, his glory, grace, and power are displayed through our infirmities and weaknesses (see 2 Corinthians 12:1-10). The time and the means of our healings—whether here on earth or in heaven—are ultimately in God's hands.

God's desire is for each person to know and follow him, to become a part of his eternal family. Sometimes God uses incredible acts of healing to draw us close to him. Other times God uses the circumstances of our lives—and others' lives—to teach and transform us into the people he made us to be for eternity. As Paul wrote, "That is why we never give up. Though our bodies are dying, our spirits are being renewed every day" (2 Corinthians 4:16).

It's only natural that we desire healing, cessation of pain, or a longer life. But we cannot forget that there is something far more important than having more days, even painless days, on this earth. There is eternity to consider—God's plan for us, one filled with *infinite possibilities*!

## Living on Higher Ground

*The Sovereign LORD is my strength!*
*He makes me as surefooted as a deer,*
*able to tread upon the heights.*

HABAKKUK 3:19

In Scripture, ascending a mountain symbolizes drawing closer to God. Moses received the Ten Commandments on Mount Sinai. Elijah called down fire to burn the sacrifice on Mount Carmel. David captured the area of Mount Zion, which was later the location of Solomon's Temple. Jesus preached the Sermon on the Mount and went up to the Mount of Transfiguration. And he went to the Mount of Olives to pray the night before his crucifixion.

These mountains were not places people normally would pass as they went about their daily routines. For the most part, they were rugged, uninhabited, barren, and potentially dangerous. At their summits, however, they provided opportunities to experience sweeping vistas of the plains below, breathtaking sunsets and sunrises, fresh breezes, and deafening silence.

The Christian life is like that too. Our obstacles can appear to tower thousands of feet over our heads. Our best efforts to climb to the summit can leave us with bruised knees and broken fingernails. Problems feel like wild animals nipping at our heels, bringing our upward climb to a halt as we wait on a scary ledge.

However, the good news of the gospel is that we don't have to stop there. God is always calling us ever higher as we spend quiet time with him and his Word. We can cry out as David did in perhaps his last song of praise to God: "You have made a wide path for my feet to keep them from slipping" (2 Samuel 22:37) and "The Lord is my rock, my fortress, and my savior" (2 Samuel 22:2). Throughout his life, David humbly acknowledged that the Lord was his source of strength and protection.

Are you waiting for God's infinite possibilities to unfold in your life? Perhaps you're tempted to "help" God get things moving. Don't do it! As David learned, even when our circumstances seem dire, we can always continue to praise God and look to him as our ultimate source of hope and protection—the One from whom our help comes (see Psalm 121:1-2).

You don't have to be alone in your hurt! Comfort *is* yours. Joy is an option. And it's all been made possible by your Savior. He went without comfort so that you might have it. He postponed joy so that you might share in it. He willingly chose isolation so that you might never be alone in your hurt and sorrow.

JONI EARECKSON TADA[3]

PART 3

# *infinite*
# TRUTH

🌿

*The Lord is my shepherd;*
*I have all that I need.*

PSALM 23:1

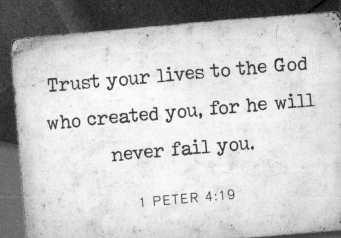

Trust your lives to the God who created you, for he will never fail you.

1 PETER 4:19

*Lord, help me trust your heart.*

Ryan shifted back and forth on his feet as the jeweler waited. Ryan had researched diamonds beforehand and knew what he wanted, but he was still apprehensive. *It has to be perfect,* he thought, *because she is perfect.* As he scanned the rows of precious stones, he knew what he could afford. After Ryan narrowed it down to two rings, the jeweler removed them from the case and delicately placed them on a swath of black velvet, a backdrop that provided contrast and enhanced the brilliance of the stones. The light danced off the angled cuts, and the diamonds sparkled even brighter than before. "That one!" Ryan proclaimed, pointing to his selection with confidence.

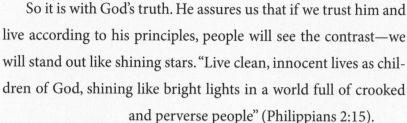

So it is with God's truth. He assures us that if we trust him and live according to his principles, people will see the contrast—we will stand out like shining stars. "Live clean, innocent lives as children of God, shining like bright lights in a world full of crooked and perverse people" (Philippians 2:15).

Have you ever seen the night sky in a place away from city lights? The same stars that were barely visible because of ambient street lights and illuminated billboards seem to pierce the darkness. As you gaze heavenward, you can't help but be inspired and awestruck by God's wondrous creation. Our daily lives, when infused with the character of God, can inspire the world around us. When we trust the Lord in the face of hardships and pain, people take notice because we "reflect the glory of the Lord. And the Lord . . . makes us more and more like him as we are changed into his glorious image" (2 Corinthians 3:18).

But how do we live as children of light during dark times? How do we maintain hope and trust in God when things don't make sense?

In his book *Shattered Dreams*,

Dr. Larry Crabb writes, "The journey to God will always, at some point, take us through darkness where life makes no sense."[1] He explains that many Christians, especially in Western cultures, don't understand God's plan for suffering:

> We will not encounter Christ as our best friend, as the source of all true goodness, as
> the One who provides the sweetest pleasure to our souls, until we abandon ourselves
> to Him. And full abandonment, real trust, rarely happens until we meet God in
> the midst of shattered dreams, until in our brokenness we see in Him the only and
> overflowingly sufficient answer to our soul's deepest cry.[2]

## Certainty in an Uncertain World

Did you ever play the "trust fall" game when you were a kid? The object of the game is to free-fall backward into the arms of a trusted friend who catches you. It's a fun but risky game—your heart races when you hear the word *go* and begin, unsure of whether your pal will really be there for you. Honestly, haven't we all had friends or family members who have let us down or broken our trust, leaving us with pain that is more severe than just landing hard on the floor?

Although people may disappoint us, the prophet Jeremiah makes it clear that we can have total confidence in God: "Blessed are those who trust in the LORD and have made the LORD their hope and confidence" (Jeremiah 17:7). Jeremiah made his bold claim while undergoing excruciating times of personal trial and suffering.

Jeremiah is just one example of someone whose faith in God never wavered. Hebrews 11 lists several biblical heroes who stood strong in the face of circumstances that would have caused many others to question their allegiance to God. They realized that "faith shows the reality of what we hope for; it is the evidence of things we cannot see" (Hebrews 11:1).

We prefer to put our hope in tangible things—a strong, healthy body; a strong financial portfolio; our country's political leaders and military power. But Proverbs offers a word of caution: "Trust in the Lord with all your heart; do not depend on your own understanding" (Proverbs 3:5).

Jeremiah saw how quickly the "elites" of his day—those with worldly power—could be brought low by the God of the universe. "Cursed are those who put their trust in mere humans, who rely on human strength and turn their hearts away from the Lord" (Jeremiah 17:5). Notice that this verse doesn't say we should not rely on others. Friends and family, especially fellow believers, are God's gifts to help us through life's challenges, to rejoice with us when we rejoice and cry with us when we cry. Jeremiah's admonishment is specifically about never turning our hearts away from the Lord, which always leads down a slippery slope. While there may be times when we need friends to catch us, our *ultimate trust* must always be in God alone.

MY GRACE IS ALL YOU NEED. MY POWER WORKS BEST IN WEAKNESS.

2 CORINTHIANS 12:9

# Trust and Obey

When I used to ride horses, I had a special relationship with my thoroughbred named Auggie. Because I fed him, brushed him, and exercised him, Auggie knew me and trusted my judgment when I guided him through his performance in the show ring. It was the joy of his heart to do my will because he trusted my wisdom. In 1 Peter 4:19 we read, "Keep on doing what is right, and trust your lives to the God who created you, for he will never fail you." We are to trust God and do what is right! Oh that we would be like a simple horse and trust the wisdom of the One holding the reins in our lives. If we'd only take the time to really know our Master (as my horse knew me), we'd trust him and obey him more easily and more faithfully.

Isaiah 1:3 says, "Even an ox knows its owner, and a donkey recognizes its master's care—but Israel doesn't know its master. My people don't recognize my care for them." We question the maze of obstacles on the course of life that the Lord sets before us. Oh sure, it may seem confusing, but God knows. And he would never place anything before us that he thought we could not handle without his grace.

*Joni*

Lord, I want to trust you with the reins of my life. You alone know what lies ahead and have the power to guide me in life's uncertainties.

_____

_____

_____

_____

_____

## *He Giveth More Grace*

When people with disabilities trust God, he is revealed as a God of supreme worth who is deserving of our love and obedience despite the pain we face. Suffering bonds Christians to the "man of sorrows" (Isaiah 53:3); we have something eternally precious in common with Christ—our afflictions. Philippians 2:6-8 says, "Though he was God, he did not think of equality with God as something to cling to. Instead . . . he humbled himself in obedience to God and died a criminal's death on a cross." Paul assures us in verse 8 that our scars, anguish, rejection, and pain give us a small taste of what our Savior endured to purchase our redemption.

Annie J. Flint experienced tremendous loss in her childhood. Her parents died when she was young, and later she lost both of her adoptive parents. She worked as a teacher until she developed arthritis that became so severe it rendered her unable to work. Although Annie supported herself as a poet, there were many days when her pain was so severe that she could not write. Her faith sustained her during such times, as evidenced by this poem, which became a favorite hymn for many after her death.

# He Giveth More Grace

LYRICS BY ANNIE JOHNSON FLINT, 1866–1932

He giveth more grace when the burden grows greater;

He sendeth more strength when the labors increase.

To added affliction He addeth His mercy;

To multiplied trials, His multiplied peace.

When we have exhausted our store of endurance,

When our strength has failed ere the day is half done,

When we reach the end of our hoarded resources,

Our Father's full giving is only begun.

> *(Refrain)*
>
> His love has no limit;
>
> His grace has no measure,
>
> His pow'r has no boundary known unto men.
>
> For out of His infinite riches in Jesus,
>
> He giveth, and giveth, and giveth again![1]

## Begin Your Day with Prayer

*You must commit yourselves wholeheartedly to these commands that I am giving you today. Repeat them again and again to your children. Talk about them when you are at home and when you are on the road, when you are going to bed and when you are getting up. Tie them to your hands and wear them on your forehead as reminders. Write them on the doorposts of your house and on your gates.*

DEUTERONOMY 6:6-9

Some truths are more important than others. The *Shema*, the creed of ancient Israel, is an ultimate truth—a truth above all others. There is one God who is the Lord. He alone is to be worshiped, and none other. The *Shema* is one of the first prayers that Jewish children learn and recite several times a day:

*Listen, O Israel! The Lord is our God, the Lord alone. And you must love the Lord your God with all your heart, all your soul, and all your strength.*

DEUTERONOMY 6:4-5

This primary truth—that the Lord our God is the Lord alone—is followed by the greatest commandment: to love the Lord with all that we are.

We need to surround ourselves with the Lord and his Word. While we may not literally write things on our foreheads or our "gates," his Word should be primary in our minds and in our homes, and we should be praying throughout each day. The New Testament instructs us to "never stop praying" (1 Thessalonians 5:17). In the morning and evening and in every sphere of life—at home, on the road, and with family and friends—we are to think and speak about God.

Many faithful Jews still recite the *Shema* daily. We can also choose to begin each day with these verses. Stopping to acknowledge who God is—the one true, all-powerful God who is Lord of our lives—and then reminding ourselves that he calls us to love him with all that we are—our strengths *and* our weaknesses—will help us to trust him, take all our concerns to him, and follow him in each situation we face.

## Count Your Blessings

Burnt toast, spilled coffee, and wrinkled clothes—some days feel destined to go poorly. When combined with life's daily struggles—a sore back, an ailing spouse, a child with special needs who requires constant attention—one can quickly spiral into despair and regret. Ever been there?

Paul could certainly identify with trying circumstances. He wrote several letters while in prison at different times, where he was in chains for preaching the gospel (see Acts 20:22-23, Ephesians 6:20, and Philippians 1:13). If anyone had reason to complain, Paul did. He endured much suffering at the hands of those who hated the message about Christ. But rather than beginning his letter to the Ephesian church with complaints, self-pity, or blame, Paul counts his blessings. His list is helpful for us as well:

*All praise to God, the Father of our Lord Jesus Christ, who has blessed us with every*
*spiritual blessing in the heavenly realms because we are united with Christ. Even*
*before he made the world, God loved us and chose us in Christ to be holy and without*

*fault in his eyes. God decided in advance to adopt us into his own family by bringing*

*us to himself through Jesus Christ. This is what he wanted to do, and it gave him great*

*pleasure. So we praise God for the glorious grace he has poured out on us who belong to*

*his dear Son. He is so rich in kindness and grace that he purchased our freedom with the*

*blood of his Son and forgave our sins. He has showered his kindness on us, along with all*

*wisdom and understanding.*

*God has now revealed to us his mysterious will regarding Christ—which is to fulfill*

*his own good plan. And this is the plan: At the right time he will bring everything*

*together under the authority of Christ—everything in heaven and on earth. Furthermore,*

*because we are united with Christ, we have received an inheritance from God, for he*

*chose us in advance, and he makes everything work out according to his plan.*

*God's purpose was that we Jews who were the first to trust in Christ would bring*

*praise and glory to God. And now you Gentiles have also heard the truth, the Good News*

*that God saves you. And when you believed in Christ, he identified you as his own by*

*giving you the Holy Spirit, whom he promised long ago. The Spirit is God's guarantee that*

*he will give us the inheritance he promised and that he has purchased us to be his own*

*people. He did this so we would praise and glorify him.*

EPHESIANS 1:3-14


Paul praises God for spiritual blessings, our adoption as children of God, forgiveness, kindness, wisdom, understanding, an inheritance, and the Holy Spirit as a guarantee of the promises of God. And that's just a start!

From the beauty of creation to the beauty of friendships, our own lists of blessings could be positively overwhelming. There is an old children's song that goes like this: "Count your blessings; name them one by one. Count your blessings; see what God has done." That is a pretty good description of what Paul is doing here in the first chapter of Ephesians. His prayer for the church at Ephesus is certainly needed for believers today:

> *I pray that your hearts will be flooded with light so that you can understand the confident hope he has given to those he called—his holy people who are his rich and glorious inheritance.*
> EPHESIANS 1:18

Why pray for light? So they could see through the darkness of life's circumstances to find hope. The next time gloom comes calling for your attention, count your blessings instead. The sun will surely break through the rain clouds, and joy will replace despair.

## Trust Your Shepherd's Heart

*Even when I walk*
*through the darkest valley,*
*I will not be afraid,*
*for you are close beside me. . . .*

*Surely your goodness and unfailing love will pursue me*
*all the days of my life.*

PSALM 23:4, 6

In this beloved psalm, David reflects on Israel's communal experience of suffering and pictures God's people as sheep in need of a loving shepherd. Just as God led the Israelites like sheep out of Egyptian slavery and walked beside them through the deep, dark, dangerous wilderness inhabited by their enemies, so he walks with his children today—even when they pass through "the darkest valley."

Under the tender care of our Good Shepherd, the Lord Jesus Christ himself (see John 10:11), we will always have everything we need (though not always everything we *want*!). He faithfully provides us with strength, guidance, discipline, protection, and—what we sometimes need most of all—rest. If you are feeling weak, aimless, undisciplined, vulnerable, or just plain tired, let God be your Shepherd. He will not disappoint.

In this life, God's children are surrounded by enemies, yet they remain safe, feasting at a table of blessings set by God himself. This is but a foretaste, a preview, of the great "wedding feast of the Lamb" (Revelation 19:9) that believers look forward to with eager anticipation, when all our enemies—including death, pain, and sorrow—will finally be vanquished once and for all. What a glorious hope!

*Find rest . . .*

Often we can't seem to find rest and peace . . . or even a way forward. This is when knowing who we are in Christ Jesus can make all the difference. Hear Jesus' words: "Come to me, all of you who are weary and carry heavy burdens, and I will give you rest. Take my yoke upon you. Let me teach you, because I am humble and gentle at heart, and you will find rest for your souls" (Matthew 11:28-29).

*Fix your thoughts . . .*

It is natural to feel anxious when we are in pain or to feel helpless while a loved one struggles. So what can we do about our anxiety and worry? Paul understood the human tendency to focus on the negative and let our thoughts spiral downward.

In Philippians 4:8, he urges us to focus our minds on things with eternal value: "Fix your thoughts on what is true, and honorable, and right, and pure, and lovely, and admirable. Think about things that are excellent and worthy of praise." This leads us into deeper spiritual territory where God can transform us. Joni's husband, Ken Tada, has been able to "fix his thoughts" on Jesus Christ and serve Joni as Christ would:

Caring for my wife, Joni, is something I gladly signed up to do on our wedding day, in sickness and in health, for better or for worse. I've learned that the secret to good caregiving is a constant awareness of one's desperate need of Jesus Christ and a steady reliance on him. When I'm serving Joni, I'm serving Jesus Christ. Caregiving may feel extremely tiring at times, but the work doesn't have to be tiresome when it's for Christ. I may get weary, but life doesn't have to be wearisome when it's all for his glory. When I minister to Joni's needs, I am serving the Savior. This truth is echoed in Matthew 25:33-42, where Jesus says if we feed the hungry, give drink to the thirsty, and clothe those in need, we are inasmuch doing it for him.[3]

When you did it to one of
the least of these
my brothers and sisters,
you were doing it to me!

MATTHEW 25:40

## God's Loving Embrace

*Unfailing love and truth have met together.*
*Righteousness and peace have kissed!*
*Truth springs up from the earth,*
*and righteousness smiles down from heaven.*

PSALM 85:10-11

Love cannot exist without truth, and peace cannot last without righteousness. These qualities are united in Christ. He bore the full weight of divine wrath against sin and paid the price on behalf of those who believe in him (see 2 Corinthians 5:21). His sacrifice made it possible for God to show peace and love to sinners and yet remain righteous and true (see Romans 3:23-26). As a result, we can rest in God's loving embrace—both now and forever.

## *Let Your Truth Be Told*

The book of Acts portrays the movement of people charged with the great commission to "go and make disciples of all the nations" (Matthew 28:18-20). It begins with Jesus leaving the earth and returning to heaven: "He was taken up into a cloud while they were watching, and they could no longer see him" (Acts 1:9). Two men in white robes appeared to the apostles, assuring them they would someday see Jesus again when he would return as he promised (see Acts 1:10-11). Afterward, his followers spread out far and wide to share the Good News about Jesus: arriving at a new place, staying for a while, and then leaving.

Life is filled with many hellos and good-byes. Our times and places have beginnings and endings. Families gather to celebrate weddings, baptisms, graduations, reunions, and relocations, as well as to grieve and mourn together at funerals. Whether briefly or for as long as we can, we must hold on to moments in life just tight enough to convey our care but loose enough to let loved ones flourish. Eventually, it's time to let go. Sometimes we don't want to leave, but we recognize it is time to move on.

In Acts 20:17-36, we're invited into the poignant moment when Paul recognized that with his future safety in question, the people in

whom he had invested so heavily would need to continue on without him. Paul told his friends they would never see him again. His farewell to the Ephesian elders was both a human and a spiritual moment—there were embraces and prayers, heartfelt commendations, pronouncements of God's blessings on one another, and benedictions:

*Guard yourselves and God's people. Feed and shepherd God's flock—his church, purchased with his own blood—over which the Holy Spirit has appointed you as leaders. . . . I entrust you to God and the message of his grace that is able to build you up and give you an inheritance with all those he has set apart for himself.*
ACTS 20:28, 32

The experience of leaving or being left is often difficult, especially when it involves leaving a loved one who has a disability; in such cases, the fear and pain can be acute and unremitting. The vulnerability of their lives; the difficulty they may have in understanding separation, loss, and death; their dependence on others; and their undetermined future can make leaving them almost unbearable. On the flip side, the fear and pain of being left can be equally crushing.

But the hope we have in the midst of departing from loved ones is built on the confidence that we're not leaving them alone—or permanently. Leaving is for this life only. In heaven, no one leaves and no one is left. And for all eternity, "The grace of the Lord Jesus [will] be with God's holy people" (Revelation 22:21).

*a word from Joni*

# Come to the Lover of Your Soul

When I approach the Lord in prayer, I relate to him in numerous ways. He's my elder Brother, the Captain of my soul, or my Friend when I need to pour out my heart to him. The Song of Songs, written by Solomon, describes the love relationship between a bridegroom and his bride—symbolically, between the Lord and his church. It portrays the Lord as the Lover of my soul: "Let me see your face; let me hear your voice. For your voice is pleasant, and your face is lovely" (Song of Songs 2:14). He inspires me to sing out my love for him.

Lord, enfold me in your everlasting arms.
Let my soul find rest and peace as I lean on
you. May doubts and cares fly away. Nothing
and no one shall ever part us. I'm yours . . .
Praise you for being mine.

_____

_____

_____

_____

_____

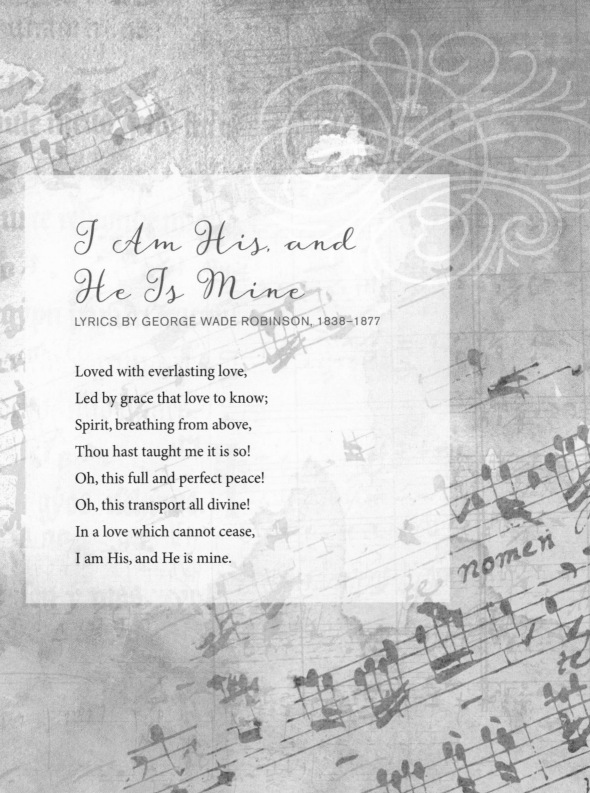

# I Am His, and He Is Mine

LYRICS BY GEORGE WADE ROBINSON, 1838–1877

Loved with everlasting love,

Led by grace that love to know;

Spirit, breathing from above,

Thou hast taught me it is so!

Oh, this full and perfect peace!

Oh, this transport all divine!

In a love which cannot cease,

I am His, and He is mine.

The PEACE
I GIVE is A GIFT
THE WORLD
CANNOT GIVE,
SO DON'T BE
TROUBLED
or
AFRAID.

JOHN 14:27

## Trust in God's Sovereignty

*As my life was slipping away, I remembered the* LORD. *And my earnest prayer went out to you in your holy Temple.*

JONAH 2:7

As he sulked in the belly of a great fish, Jonah was searching for ways to describe how helpless he felt in the situation he was facing. But even in the depths of despair, he remembered to call out to the Lord (see Jonah 1:17–2:10).

With the right perspective, we can learn to praise God no matter what life brings, because God is still King of all kings and wants to save his children. We can trust him to care for his people.

Satan uses our fear against us, causing us to doubt God's goodness and provision. When God *feels* distant, we must cling to his promises. In an interview with the *Christian Post*, Pastor Rick Warren points out that there are 365 times in the Bible where God encourages us to "fear not." Warren says, "Our hurts and hang-ups can often cause us to think that God is out to get us, that all He wants to do is condemn us and punish us. But that simply isn't true."[4]

Katie Jo Ramsey is a therapist and writer who struggles with chronic pain from an autoimmune disease. In an article for *Christianity Today*, she shares how her vulnerability has taught her that God has hardwired us to need him and others:

> Where our culture heralds individual sufficiency and autonomy, suffering reminds me
> I am inadequate to face disease and disappointment on my own. I am not enough, and
> I was never intended to be sufficient to meet my own needs. . . .

Perhaps that is the gift of suffering: It forces us to realize we cannot bear the pain of life on our own. When I allow my suffering to be seen and received by others, my brain learns how to trust. Ultimately, relationships of shared brokenness teach my brain to rely on the only Person who can and will redeem the pain so rampant in my body and this world. My brain, like my body and soul, was made to crave relationships. In my suffering, I know I need others. More importantly, I know I need God.[5]

Is there a special friend who has been there to share your brokenness and pain? Take time to thank God for him or her. Then reflect on someone who may need your support today.

## Two Miracles

Asking others for help is humbling and can be life changing for everyone involved. If the person you ask has little to give, your request may seem selfish or insensitive. But what if God has *told* you to ask that person for assistance?

In 1 Kings 17:8-9, the prophet Elijah receives a word from God directing him to go to Zarephath, where he would meet an impoverished widow and single mother who had no way of knowing that God was about to set in motion a miracle—one that would not only provide for her needs but also impact her faith forever. This story plays out in three acts.

*Act One (verses 10-16):* Elijah instructs the widow to use her meager supplies of flour and cooking oil to bake some bread to feed him first, then herself and her son. Elijah acts with God's assurance that there will be enough food from that day until the new rains arrive and the crops grow. The widow follows the prophet's instructions, and there is enough flour and oil to meet their daily needs. The promise of God is fulfilled.

*Act Two (verses 17-22):* When the widow's son becomes sick and dies, the desperate woman turns to Elijah for help. He carries the child to his own room and prays. His first prayer is a complaint: "Why bring this tragedy on a poor woman who is simply struggling to stay alive? How can this be fair?" His second prayer is a request: "Give back the child's life" (verses 20-21, paraphrased). And God does.

*Act Three (verses 23-24):* The grieving mother is given back a healthy, living son. Her response goes beyond simple joy or relief—she acknowledges the activity of God in the life and words of his prophet.

Elijah was obedient, willing to trust God and humble himself to ask for help, even when it made no sense. The result? An abundant provision came through an unlikely source, and a struggling woman's faith was strengthened.

It's easy to celebrate God's miracles and provision, but what happens if God says no? How do we respond when God seems silent in response to our prayers?

Wrestling with similar questions, Philip Yancey wrote *Reaching for the Invisible God.* He points to Jeremiah's exhortation that those who trust God "are like trees planted along a riverbank, with roots that reach deep into the water. Such trees are not bothered by the heat or worried by long months of drought. Their leaves stay green, and they never stop producing fruit" (Jeremiah 17:8). As Yancey explains,

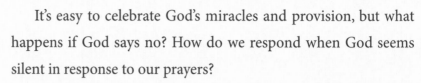

> The Bible makes no rosy promises about living only in springtime. Instead, it points toward faith that helps us prepare for arid seasons. Harsh winters will come, followed by scorching summers. Yet if the roots of faith go deep enough, tapping into Living Water, we can survive the drought times and flourish in times of plenty.[6]

## Trusting Anyway

*But even if he doesn't . . .*

DANIEL 3:18

Shadrach, Meshach, and Abednego were young Israelite men who had been captured and taken to Babylon. When they refused to bow down to the gold statue King Nebuchadnezzar had made, he threatened to lock them inside a fiery furnace. The three brave men proclaimed to the king that though their Lord could rescue them, their faith in God did not depend on being rescued. Their words "but even if he doesn't" affirmed their faith in a God whose ways are not our ways (see Daniel 3 and Isaiah 55:9).

For some, the diagnosis of a disabling condition can feel like being thrown into a fire that could consume the life they once knew. It can cause them to question their faith. Do they still believe God is able to deliver them? If God has the power to remove suffering but chooses not to, can they trust his sovereignty and goodness?

When parents of a special-needs child receive the life-altering diagnosis, they may ask, "Do we believe that God can heal our child? Do we have enough faith?" If God does not bring physical healing, they may struggle, asking, "Do we need more faith?"

When Ashley received the diagnosis of her son's rare genetic disorder, she knew life would never be the same. But God met her in her fear and sadness and slowly began to reveal his presence in small ways. Ashley's heart began to trust that having a child with special needs was not going to destroy her faith. She prayed for more confidence to trust God. She clung to the hope that even if the circumstances weren't what she would have chosen for her child, God would keep them on the best path for their lives. Ashley also prayed that others would see God's sustaining presence through her family.

Where does your heart go when God does not rescue you from difficult circumstances? Do you run toward fear and doubt, or do you turn to God? Remember, you're never alone—God is with you. Walk by faith on your uphill journey with this motto: "But even if he doesn't, I will trust in his goodness and love."

How is God asking you to trust him today? What *infinite truth* do you need to lean into to find comfort?

When you are on the mountaintop, it's easy to say, "Oh yes, I believe God can do it," but you have to come down from the mountain to the demon-possessed valley and face the realities that scoff at your Mount-of-Transfiguration belief (see Luke 9:28-42). . . .

There is continual testing in the life of faith up to the point of our physical death, which is the last great test. Faith is absolute trust in God—trust that could never imagine that He would forsake us (see Hebrews 13:5-6).[7]

OSWALD CHAMBERS

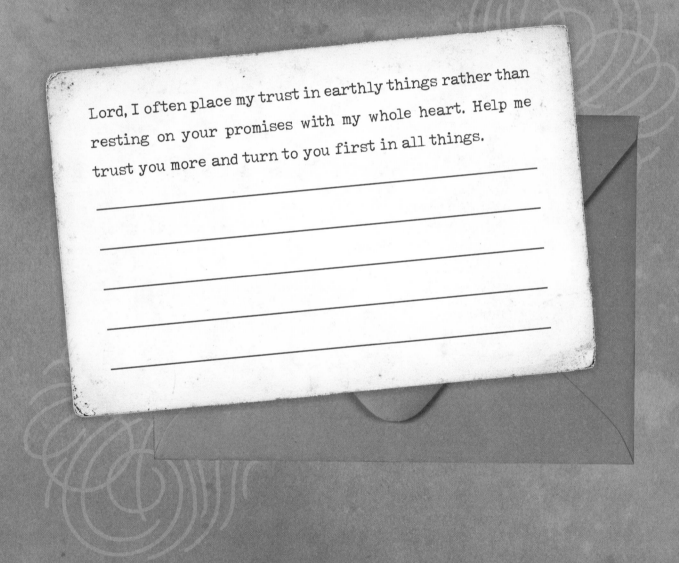

Lord, I often place my trust in earthly things rather than resting on your promises with my whole heart. Help me trust you more and turn to you first in all things.

_____

_____

_____

_____

_____

PART 4

*infinite*

TOMORROWS

❦

*It is finished! I am the Alpha and the Omega—*
*the Beginning and the End. To all who are thirsty I*
*will give freely from the springs of the water of life. All*
*who are victorious will inherit all these blessings, and*
*I will be their God, and they will be my children.*

REVELATION 21:6-7

We are looking forward
to the new heavens and
new earth he has promised.

2 PETER 3:13

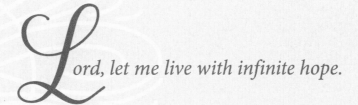

*ord, let me live with infinite hope.*

CHILDREN DON'T LIKE TO WAIT. Whether it's a road trip to see their grandparents—*Are we there yet?*—or waiting for a special package to arrive, their impatience is palpable. We offer them assurances of the joy to come and clarify expectations, but the waiting is still tough. As adults, many of us still struggle with delayed gratification and perseverance. Add suffering into the equation, and looking ahead can seem almost too much to bear.

## Your Suffering Will End

Think back to a time when you eagerly awaited something wonderful that you knew was ahead. Waiting was only possible—and worth it—because you were assured it was coming. Scripture repeatedly assures us that because of what Jesus Christ has done for us, our own sufferings will eventually come to an end. Jesus has removed our sin, so now we can live in joyful and eager anticipation of the day when he will remove all pain and suffering and our salvation will be complete (see Hebrews 9:24-28).

The apostle Paul understood keenly that he had not yet arrived at his "final destination"—he was, as we might put it today, "just passin' through." As Paul explained, "We know that when this earthly tent we live in is taken down (that is, when we die and leave this earthly body), we will have a house in heaven, an eternal body made for us by God himself and not by human hands" (2 Corinthians 5:1). For now, though, "we grow weary in our present bodies, and we long to put on our heavenly bodies like new clothing" (2 Corinthians 5:2). Still, in light of Christ's resurrection, Paul could remain steadfastly confident that even if his sufferings led to death, something far greater was in store for him. Our earthly bodies grow weary, and we all long for the day when Christ will give us heavenly bodies to put on. With this eternal perspective, we, too, can live for Christ every day as we await our ultimate re-creation.

Amazingly, we not only have new, glorified bodies to look forward to but also "are looking forward to the new heavens and new earth [God] has promised, a world filled with [his] righteousness" (2 Peter 3:13). In heaven, we will see no disease or disability, no suffering or shame. Instead, we will have sturdy legs and will run and dance with the Lord. We will have strong voices to sing his praises. Our minds will be sharp and able to understand quickly, and we will gaze upon his glorious face with crystal-clear vision. And though seemingly incomprehensible now, as our sufferings pass away we will be able to declare with confidence, "It was worth it all along!"

World-renowned author, preacher, and evangelist Billy Graham spent his life inviting millions to give their lives to Jesus Christ as their Lord and Savior. In his later years, his writings focused on heaven as our joyous hope. Unfortunately, not everyone shares this hope. In his book *Nearing Home*, Rev. Graham recalls a letter he received from a young man who believed that "life after death is just a myth." In response, Rev. Graham said, "Your letter deeply saddened me, . . . because it means you are living without hope—hope for this life, and hope for the life to come. Have you honestly faced how empty and meaningless this will make your life?"[1] He went on to encourage the young man to turn his life over to Jesus Christ and find the hope that God had planned for him all along. Aptly enough, the hymn "Take My Life" was often sung at Billy Graham crusades around the world.

# Take My Life

LYRICS BY FRANCES RIDLEY HAVERGAL (1836–1879)

Take my life and let it be
Consecrated, Lord, to Thee;
Take my moments and my days—
Let them flow in ceaseless praise,
Let them flow in ceaseless praise.

Take my hands, and let them move
At the impulse of Thy love;
Take my feet and let them be
Swift and beautiful for Thee,
Swift and beautiful for Thee.

Take my voice and let me sing
Always, only, for my King;
Take my lips and let them be
Filled with messages from Thee,
Filled with messages from Thee.

Take my silver and my gold—
Not a mite would I withhold;
Take my intellect and use
Ev'ry pow'r as Thou shalt choose,
Ev'ry pow'r as Thou shalt choose.

Take my will and make it Thine—
It shall be no longer mine;
Take my heart—it is Thine own,
It shall be Thy royal throne,
It shall be Thy royal throne.

Take my love—my Lord, I pour
At Thy feet its treasure store;
Take myself—and I will be
Ever, only, all for Thee,
Ever, only, all for Thee.

Lord, I give you my life, my hands, my voice, and my will today. If I've withheld any part of myself from you, show it to me. Thank you for the treasures you have prepared for me for all eternity.

_____

_____

_____

_____

*This is how God loved the world: He gave his one and only Son, so that everyone who believes in him will not perish but have eternal life.*

JOHN 3:16

## Dancing after Catastrophe

Trapped for more than twenty-five hours under concrete tangled with wood and metal from a devastating earthquake, a young woman's body lay crushed and bleeding. She was a dance teacher who, along with her baby, lived with her mother-in-law. As she lay suffering in the darkness, she wondered if she would live—let alone dance again.

Zhi Liao did survive the earthquake that struck the Sichuan province of China in May 2008. But she lost her infant daughter, her mother-in-law, and her legs. Both legs were amputated below the knees in order to extract Zhi from the rubble. An estimated 70,000 people died that day, and 374,000 were injured. Zhi was the only one to survive in the building that she was in.

Tragedies like this prompt questions about God's goodness. If God is sovereign and in control of all things, why are there horrific natural disasters? Why does a good God allow a child to be taken from his or her mother? Why is there such dreadful suffering? Think of the great flood described in Genesis, the natural disaster where only Noah and his family were spared. Noah "walked in close fellowship with God" (Genesis 6:9) before the rain began. This relationship sustained Noah's faith through the disaster and helped him face the daunting task of making a new life after the flood had devastated the earth. Yes, Noah had learned to trust God in every circumstance. And the end of Noah's trial was marked by God's sign of a rainbow, promising that he would never again flood the entire earth.

Zhi (who has adopted the English name "Jollie") also learned to trust Christ despite her harrowing ordeal and accepted him as her Savior. She also received the precious gift of two prosthetic legs that allowed her to continue dancing. Today, Zhi travels the world using her artistic expression as both a witness to her faith and an inspiration to people with disabilities![2]

Like Noah's rainbow, Zhi's life radiates the vibrant colors of God's promise. Noah's and Zhi's courageous faith reassures us that while we may not find all the answers to our questions, we can trust God's love even in the midst of unspeakable catastrophes.

"For I know the plans I have for you," says the LORD. "They are plans for good and not for disaster, to give you a future and a hope."

JEREMIAH 29:11

# God's Plan for You

Don't you love thinking about old times? The older I get, the more I enjoy reflecting on memories, talking about favorite vacations and childhood jaunts, and remembering my dear mother, who is now in heaven. My sweetest memories are those that inspire hope. I recall what it was like to peel an orange, pluck a guitar, hold a cold glass of Coke, and feel my fingers tap the cool piano keys.

Why do such memories inspire hope for me? Because rather than making me lament for what once was, I let them remind me that one day I will have new hands. My new fingers might dig in the dirt and pick and scrub fresh vegetables. And I smile as I imagine holding the hand of my dear husband, Ken, in heaven someday.

My best memories give shape to that hopeful future promised in Jeremiah 29:11. Your memories—especially if you've lost a loved one, or your health, or your ability to think clearly—should inspire hope in you, too. As wonderful as the world was when all those special remembrances occurred—as wonderful as it was when my hands worked—these things are only a foretaste of more delightful, pleasurable experiences to come. Jesus is the One who makes our futures bright. Jesus assures us that our best memories will one day blossom into a more joyous reality than we can ever imagine. He is our hope (see 1 Timothy 1:1).

What are your memories of things lost? How might those memories inspire hope in you today? How might those remembrances draw you closer to Jesus, the God of all hope? Grab hold of Jeremiah 29:11—and so many other Scriptures that promise the world. Oh, not this world, but the world to come!

*Lord of hope, thank you for the promise of a future and a hope.*
*Amen.*

THE SCRIPTURES GIVE us HOPE & ENCOURAGEMENT AS WE WAIT PATIENTLY FOR GOD'S PROMISES to be FULFILLED.

ROMANS 15:4

## God Will Dry Your Tears

This life is filled with sadness and tears when our bodies are wracked by diseases or disabilities or when we struggle financially. Friends and loved ones pass away—sometimes unexpectedly, and often much too soon. On this side of eternity, we grieve. But if we have placed our faith in Jesus Christ, we do not grieve without hope (see 1 Thessalonians 4:13-15). Indeed, Scripture pulls the curtains of history back just far enough for us to catch a glimpse of a reality in which our present difficulties give way to a glorious eternity in which there are no more tears or pain. Revelation 7:17 tells us that "the Lamb on the throne will be their Shepherd. He will lead them to springs of life-giving water. And God will wipe every tear from their eyes." This beautiful passage combines images from several Old Testament passages: The Lamb is also the Shepherd of Psalm 23; and in fulfillment of the promise in Isaiah 25:8, God will gently wipe away the streaming tears of the faithful witnesses who endured persecution unto death. There will be no more pain, suffering, hunger, or thirst—they (and we!) will dwell in the house of the Lord forever.

> I saw the holy city, the new Jerusalem, coming down from God out of heaven . . .
>    I heard a loud shout from the throne, saying, "Look, God's home is now among his people! He will live with them, and they will be his people. God himself will be with them."
>
> REVELATION 21:2-3

Suffering will eventually come to an end. In the meantime, faithfulness to God and his Word are the keys to remaining in fellowship with the Father and the Son. It is in the sweetness of that fellowship that we get a foretaste of the eternal life that we will forever enjoy with him.

## Rejoicing in Lament

As the professor ascended the podium, his students expected another lecture on theology; instead, he was about to make theology come alive. This forty-year-old teacher was about to tell his students that he had recently been diagnosed with a rare, incurable cancer.

The professor was J. Todd Billings, research professor of Reformed theology at Western Theological Seminary. During the time he had left on earth, Billings wanted to educate his students—and the church—on what it meant to live out the theology of suffering he had taught for so long. So in 2015, he published a book titled *Rejoicing in Lament: Wrestling with Incurable Cancer and Life in Christ.*

How do we *rejoice* in lament? The book of Jeremiah gives us a hint. At its core is God's promise to one day establish a "new covenant" with his people, in which he will write his laws "on their hearts" (see Jeremiah 31:31-34). He will be their God, and they will be his people— enjoying sweet, unbroken fellowship with him forever.

Centuries later, Jesus Christ instituted that new covenant through the shedding of his blood on the cross, making it possible for broken humanity to be reconciled with their Maker. Because of this, we can look forward with eager anticipation to the renewal of all creation, including our bodies—the same bodies that now sometimes suffer from rare, incurable cancers. In the meantime, we have the presence of Christ and his indwelling Spirit, which gives us a sustaining hope.

That hope, in turn, empowers us to rejoice in the midst of lament. For we know that God, when he makes all things new, "will not forget the blind and lame," nor anyone else who suffers (Jeremiah 31:8). Instead, "the young women will dance for joy, and the men—old and young— will join in the celebration," and God himself "will turn their mourning into joy" (verse 13).

As the title of Billings's book suggests, rejoicing in the midst of lament is made possible in the context of a vibrant, living relationship with Jesus Christ. For Billings, there will come a day when he will no longer stand behind the lectern. Instead, he will stand behind the torn curtain (see Hebrews 9:3 and Matthew 27:51) as he awaits the blessed hope of the appearance of our great God and Savior, Jesus Christ (see Titus 2:12-13)—and he will lament no more. There will only be rejoicing.

Despite all these things, overwhelming victory is ours through Christ, who loved us.

ROMANS 8:37

*Now our knowledge is partial and incomplete. . . . But when the time of perfection comes, these partial things will become useless. . . .*

*Now we see things imperfectly, like puzzling reflections in a mirror, but then we will see everything with perfect clarity. . . . I will know everything completely, just as God now knows me completely.*

*Three things will last forever—faith, hope, and love—and the greatest of these is love.*
1 CORINTHIANS 13:9-13 (EMPHASIS ADDED)

## Our Great Reward

Have you suffered terribly? Perhaps it has been from disease or disability. Perhaps you have suffered exclusion in school or work situations or even in your family. Maybe you have come alongside those who have suffered in this manner and have shared their suffering. If so, you walk with many millions of Jesus' followers around the world, today and throughout the ages, who have been persecuted because of their faith. In the twentieth century alone, large numbers of Christians under ruthless dictators faced imprisonment, the loss of belongings and homes, and even death because they claimed the name of Christ.

Whether in response to one's physical condition or one's religious faith, experiencing public ridicule, shame, and oppression can be almost unbearable. How does one hold up under such suffering, especially if it persists for years on end? The original audience of the book of Hebrews were fellow sufferers. How did they make it? The secret is in Hebrews 10:34. Those who suffer while believing in Christ can endure because they know that there are "better things waiting for [them] that will last forever." Jesus spoke about these "better things" in the Beatitudes (see Matthew 5:3-12). Those who continue to believe, even when—and especially when—they suffer, will receive comfort, justice, mercy, blessing, and ultimate satisfaction through fellowship with God in Christ.

Whatever struggles you are facing, may the knowledge of our future great reward yield a "confident trust" (Hebrews 10:35). Let us continue to live with "patient endurance" (verse 36) so that we can receive what God has promised. "Come, Lord Jesus!" (Revelation 22:20).

## You Have an Inheritance

We all battle the enemies of discouragement and disappointment, especially when we are in emotional or physical pain. These enemies can cause a tremendous amount of suffering. When facing these enemies, nothing lifts our spirits quite like reflecting on the promises of God's Kingdom and our glorious future with him. Scripture abounds with reminders of these promises. In 1 Corinthians, the apostle Paul assures us,

> We will not all die, but we will all be transformed! It will happen in a moment, in the blink of an eye, when the last trumpet is blown. For when the trumpet sounds, those who have died will be raised to live forever. And we who are living will also be transformed. For our dying bodies must be transformed into bodies that will never die; our mortal bodies must be transformed into immortal bodies.
>
> Then, when our dying bodies have been transformed into bodies that will never die, this Scripture will be fulfilled:
>
> "Death is swallowed up in victory.
> O death, where is your victory?
> O death, where is your sting?"
>
> For sin is the sting that results in death, and the law gives sin its power. But thank God! He gives us victory over sin and death through our Lord Jesus Christ.
>
> 1 CORINTHIANS 15:51-57

There will come a day when our bodies that were once buried in weakness will be raised to live in strength (see 1 Corinthians 15:40-44). What a glorious truth that brings encouragement

to our souls! It was good news to the believers in Corinth, and it is good news to us today. This is our hope! This is our life! This is our Christ!

This future destiny was made possible by Jesus Christ, our Lord and Savior. Because he died for us, we inherit his righteousness, his imperishable and indestructible life (Hebrews 7:16). Though our earthly bodies change and decay, we can still look forward to a priceless inheritance. In heaven, we will be free from disease and the deterioration of age—free from the limitations placed on us by our earthly bodies. In the meantime, living in a godly manner despite our suffering showcases genuine faith. In fact, suffering can be the very thing that refines our faith and attracts others to the family of God.

> So, my dear brothers and sisters, be strong and immovable. Always work enthusiastically for the Lord, for you know that nothing you do for the Lord is ever useless.
>
> 1 CORINTHIANS 15:58

## Hope in the Midst of Struggles

The apostle Paul begins Romans 5 with the presupposition that we have peace with God. This is not a simplistic assertion by Paul. He has taken four chapters to explain both the need for being right with God (see Romans 1:18–3:20) and the way to get right with God (see Romans 3:21–4:25). Having carefully built his argument, Paul has arrived at the settled conclusion that peace with God is a reality.

Getting right with God, according to Paul, is based on faith—the kind of faith that Abraham, the father of faith, demonstrated (see Romans 4:3). It is not based on the law or perfect behavior or perfect bodies. There are no qualifications or exemptions here—no matter how much we might feel that somehow we are the exceptions to the rule. We think, *Surely God wouldn't accept me.* We reprimand ourselves for our failures and our imperfectly functioning bodies. We think that if only we had not failed God in our heads, our hearts, and our whole physical being, we could find peace with God.

But that is not what Paul writes. Since we have been made right with God—no exceptions—we already have peace with God. Moreover, we have this peace because of our faith in what Jesus did for us. It had nothing to do with our heads or our hearts or our bodies in the first place. If this is true—and it is—what are we to do with our agonizing, unrelenting pain? Does the peace we have with God make the circumstances of our lives simply vanish? Certainly not. We can simultaneously have pain and peace.

Christ experienced pain and suffering in order to reconcile us to God—not because we were perfect, but because we were broken. Christ died for us, imperfect though we are. God saw our intense suffering and entered into it with us. Because of this, we have the assurance that even during trials we have peace with God.

Steve Bundy[3] found this divine peace one night in a "burning bush" moment with God. Caring for his son, Caleb, had left Steve emotionally and physically exhausted. He was tired of asking God questions about Caleb's severe developmental disabilities and getting no answers. His grief and depression resulted partly from Caleb's irregular sleep patterns and partly from his church's beliefs that healing was for all—no exceptions. They prayed for Steve's faith to increase and his sin to be confessed so his son would be healed. But when Caleb was not healed, Steve struggled with why God's favor did not rest on him and his family.

One night when Caleb was two, he awoke crying, and Steve went to his room to comfort him until he went back to sleep. As Caleb dozed off, Steve lay on the floor, asking God why he had not *fixed* Caleb. That's when God's presence filled the room and awakened Steve's soul. He shares his story:

While I didn't hear an audible voice, these words flooded my heart and mind: *Son, aren't you glad that I didn't require you to be fixed before I accepted you?* I couldn't move or speak. In a watershed moment, I felt the unconditional love of my heavenly Father burst into my soul. There I was praying for Caleb's brokenness to be fixed, and instead, I came to grips with my own brokenness. God accepted me not because of my worth or goodness. It is because of his love and goodness that I can cry out with confidence, "Abba, Father . . . Daddy!"

With tears running down my cheeks, I held my sleeping son in my arms and said, "Caleb, I love you just the way you are, and I don't need you to be fixed. You are my son, and I'll love you unconditionally from this day forth, whether or not you are ever healed." That moment changed my life.[4]

## You Will Share His Glory

*Then I saw a new heaven and a new earth, for the old heaven and the old earth had disappeared. And the sea was also gone. And I saw the holy city, the new Jerusalem, coming down from God out of heaven like a bride beautifully dressed for her husband.*

*I heard a loud shout from the throne, saying, "Look, God's home is now among his people! He will live with them, and they will be his people. God himself will be with them. He will wipe every tear from their eyes, and there will be no more death or sorrow or crying or pain. All these things are gone forever."*

*And the one sitting on the throne said, "Look, I am making everything new!" And then he said to me, "Write this down, for what I tell you is trustworthy and true." And he also said, "It is finished! I am the Alpha and the Omega—the Beginning and the End. To all who are thirsty I will give freely from the springs of the water of life. All who are victorious will inherit all these blessings, and I will be their God, and they will be my children.*

REVELATION 21:1-7

This vision of our promised redemption takes our breath away—a new heaven and a new earth without death, pain, suffering, and sadness, where God dwells with his people. How will our new bodies work? We are not given many details. But John, the author of the book of Revelation, is clear that the crucified and risen Lamb, the Beginning and the End, is the One making all things new. We should put our trust in him.

How should we live in light of this knowledge of our future destiny? Scripture encourages us to "run the race" well:

*Since we are surrounded by such a huge crowd of witnesses to the life of faith, let us strip off every weight that slows us down, especially the sin that so easily trips us up. And let us run with endurance the race God has set before us. We do this by keeping our eyes on Jesus, the champion who initiates and perfects our faith. Because of the joy awaiting him, he endured the cross, disregarding its shame. Now he is seated in the place of honor beside God's throne.*

HEBREWS 12:1-2

Some people see life as a rat race—constant movement with no point and no good end. But as believers in Christ, we can run our races with our eyes on the finish line, where Jesus waits to embrace us. He is your champion. Untold thousands in heaven are cheering for you today! Ask God for his joy as you run your race so that those around you will be drawn to your life of faith.

## The Anchor Holds

The book of Acts records the golden days of Paul's ministry. It seemed effortless for him and Silas to be wide awake at midnight in a jail cell, praying and singing hymns at the top of their lungs despite their biting chains. Suddenly there was an earthquake, and the jail doors flew open and everyone's chains fell off. But none of the prisoners escaped. The jail keeper—amazed at what had happened—asked Paul and Silas how to be saved. He and his family received the Lord, and he invited Paul and Silas to his house (see Acts 16:16-34). Things were looking up!

But if you look at Paul's final epistle, 2 Timothy, you see another side—a harder side. Paul was in jail again when he penned this letter. But this time there was no miracle, no escape. Winter was approaching, and Paul felt old and tired. Deserted by his friends, he struggled against sickness. His friend Trophimus was also sick, yet Paul couldn't do a thing to heal his friend. He couldn't even heal himself! Still, the old apostle didn't allow discouraging circumstances to get him down. Things were different than in the golden days of old, yet he courageously hung on to God (see 2 Timothy 4:6-22).

Some days life is on the upswing; other days it's flat. Sometimes you sense the miracles in your life; other times life seems very ordinary. Are you energized today to meet a challenge head-on? Or do you feel tired and trapped? Life's circumstances can make you feel like a yo-yo, but don't allow the ups and downs to discourage you. Commit to God to fight the good fight, finish the race, and keep the faith (see verse 7). Can you learn to trust the One who is the anchor for your soul?

*Give me strength, Lord, to finish well and not allow life's disappointments—along with age, aches, and pains—to dampen my trust.*

No EYE HAS SEEN, NO EAR HAS HEARD WHAT GOD HAS PREPARED FOR THOSE WHO LOVE HIM.

1 CORINTHIANS 2:9

## *Run On in Faith!*

Eighteen individuals are specifically mentioned in Hebrews 11, also known as the "Hall of Faith," but there are many more saints who go unnamed (see verses 2, 29-30, and 32-38). What did they have in common? They all believed "that God exists and that he rewards those who sincerely seek him" (verse 6). Furthermore, the vast majority were ordinary, obscure people who lived with faith in mundane places, usually receiving little or no notice from the world at large. Yet the impact of their faith had ripple effects even centuries later in God's providential plan.

These faithful followers of the God of Israel all died without having received all that was promised to them. Despite their difficult, seemingly insignificant lives, they continued to believe that God saw them. They believed God governed the world and would ultimately make things right. In fact, the writer of Hebrews says, "They were too good for this world" (verse 38) and "God had something better in mind" both for us and for them (verse 40).

Let that thought sink in. God considered these unnamed people—little known in their own time and still unknown today—"too good for this world"; yet they had treasures in heaven waiting to be inherited on the last day.

Can you see yourself in this great company of saints? Your life may seem insignificant by all measures of worldly power and influence. But God does not do things the way the world expects. He humbles the proud and mighty, and he exalts the lowly and despised. God sees your suffering, and because he chose to be incarnated as a human being, he feels your pain. In his divine plan, he will reward you for believing that he is real, and he holds a place for you in heaven because you trust in Jesus as your Savior. Believe this promise of God as so many have before you. These unknown saints of old are part of that "huge crowd of witnesses to the life of faith" (Hebrews 12:1), and they are cheering you on in your race. Run on by faith!

# Joy Craves a Crowd

Misery may love company, but joy craves a crowd. The Father, the Son, and the Holy Spirit long to fill the hearts of thirsty people who are spiritually dehydrated from a lack of joy. The Father is gathering an inheritance of people who will join him in the river of joy that is heaven. He is heaven-bent on gathering glad souls who will make it their eternal ambition to worship his Son in the joy of the Holy Spirit.

God is love, and the wish of love is to drench with delight those who have stepped into the fellowship of sharing in his Son's suffering. And soon, the Father, the Son, and the Holy Spirit are going to get their wish. Perhaps sooner than we think, God will close the curtain on sin, suffering, disease, and death, and we will step under a veritable Niagara Falls of thunderous joy.

I may have suffered with Christ on earth, but one day in heaven I'm going to reign with him. I may have tasted the pains of living on this planet, but one day I'm going to eat from the tree of life in the pleasure of heaven. There we will feel utterly at home, as though it were always this way, as though we were born for such a place—and we were!

In a way, I hope I can bring my wheelchair to heaven. I know that's not theologically correct, but I hope I can wheel it up to Jesus, hold his nail-pierced hands, and say, "Jesus, see this wheelchair? You were right when you said that in this world we would have trouble. This wheelchair was a lot of trouble. But the weaker I was in it, the harder I leaned on you. And the harder I leaned on you, the stronger I discovered you to be. Thank you for giving me this bruising of a blessing. My wheelchair showed me a side of your grace that I never would have seen otherwise."

Then the real ticker tape parade of praise will begin! All of earth's redeemed will join in the party when Christ opens our eyes to the great fountain of joy in his heart that is beyond all we have ever experienced on earth. And when we're able to stop laughing and crying, the Lord Jesus really *will* wipe away our tears. I find it so poignant that at the point when I finally do have the use of my arms to wipe away my own tears, I won't even have to. God will wipe them away for me. And he will do the same for you.

When struggles seem endless

and the journey is long,

focus on God's gift of HOPE—

Accept its infinite assurance . . .

See its infinite possibilities . . .

Search for its infinite truth . . .

Live out

hope's infinite

tomorrows.

Lord, I choose to live beyond my suffering and the chains of this world. I choose to soar beyond the depths of my sorrows to new heights with you. I believe in your eternal plan for me and for my loved ones. Praise your precious name.

_____

_____

_____

_____

# NOTES

**PART 2: INFINITE POSSIBILITIES**

1. Ann Voskamp, *One Thousand Gifts Devotional: Reflections on Finding Everyday Graces* (Grand Rapids, MI: Zondervan, 2012), 66.

2. Megan's story is used by permission of her parents, Wayne and Kathie Moss. Learn more about Megan's story at http://www.cnn.com/2017/06/30/health/heart-transplant-survivor-dies-after-giving-birth-trnd/index.html.

3. Joni Eareckson Tada, *Glorious Intruder: God's Presence in Life's Chaos* (Colorado Springs: Multnomah, 2011), 48.

**PART 3: INFINITE TRUTH**

1. Larry Crabb, *Shattered Dreams: God's Unexpected Path to Joy* (Colorado Springs: WaterBrook, 2001), 155.

2. Ibid., 172–73.

3. Adapted from Ken Tada, "Caregiving: A Cause for Christ," *Tabletalk* magazine, October 1, 2011, Ligonier Ministries, http://www.ligonier.org/learn/articles/caregiving-a-cause-for-christ/.

4. Katherine Weber, "Rick Warren: Why God Encourages Christians to 'Fear Not' 365 Times in the Bible," *Christian Post*, April 30, 2016, https://www.christianpost.com/news/rick-warren-why-god-encourages-christians-to-fear-not-365-times-in-the-bible-163029/.

5. Katie Jo Ramsey, "God Made Our Brains to Need Others," *Christianity Today*, October 2017, http://www.christianitytoday.com/women/2017/october/god-made-our-brains-to-need-others.html.

6. Philip Yancey, *Reaching for the Invisible God: What Can We Expect to Find?* (Grand Rapids, MI: Zondervan, 2000), 74.

7. Oswald Chambers, *My Utmost for His Highest: An Updated Edition in Today's Language* (Grand Rapids, MI: Discovery House, 1992), August 29 entry. Orig. pub. by Dodd, Mead & Company, 1935.

**PART 4: INFINITE TOMORROWS**

1. Billy Graham, *Nearing Home: Life, Faith, and Finishing Well* (Nashville, TN: Thomas Nelson, 2011), 167.

2. China Source Team, "Learning to Love after the Earthquake," CHINASOURCE, July 7, 2015, https://www.chinasource.org/resource-library/chinese-church-voices/learning-to-love-after-the-earthquake. Videos of Jollie can be found on Joni's blog at http://www.joniandfriends.org/blog/story-china/?page=3.

3. Steve Bundy's story is adapted from Joni and Friends, *Real Families, Real Needs: A Compassionate Guide for Families Living with Disability* (Colorado Springs: Focus on the Family, 2017), 8–10.

4. Steve Bundy, "Does My Son Need to Be Healed?" in *Beyond Suffering Study Guide: A Christian View on Disability Ministry*, by Joni Eareckson Tada and Steve Bundy with Pat Verbal (Agoura Hills, CA: Joni and Friends, 2012), 2–3.

# SCRIPTURE INDEX

# ART BY JONI EARECKSON TADA

**THE LIGHTHOUSE**
Oil paint
*cover, 42*

**MY FATHER'S CREATION–
THE WOOD CARVER**
Pastel pencil
*8*

**SNOW PINE AND FENCE**
Pen and ink
*10*

**SHEEP GATE**
Pen and ink
*11*

**JESUS' BAPTISM**
Oil paint; a collaboration with
James Sewell
*14*

# ART BY JONI EARECKSON TADA, CONTINUED

**GIRL SITTING AT BEACH**
Pen and ink
*16*

**MARY AND BABY JESUS 1**
Pastel pencil
*17*

**AFTERNOON AT YOSEMITE**
Watercolor
*20*

**WATERFALL AND JOHN 7:38**
Pen and ink
*27*

**LIGHT IN THE FOREST**
Mixed media
*47*

**FACE OF ANGUISH**
Charcoal pencil
*50*

**ROCK OF AGES**
Watercolor
*55*

**DEER IN WOODS**
Pen and ink
*56*

**PATH TO BETHLEHEM**
Oil paint
*60*

**HORSE IN WILD MUSTARD–
DAPPLE GRAY**
Watercolor and acrylic
*65*

# ART BY JONI EARECKSON TADA, CONTINUED

**SERMON ON THE MOUNT**
Oil paint
*71*

**GOLDEN TULIPS AND IRIS**
Watercolor, pen and ink
*75*

**PRAISING GOD**
Pen and ink
*78*

**MOUNTAIN MAJESTY**
Watercolor
*82*

**SHADY TREE**
Pen and ink
*84*

**MAILBOX AND ROSES**
Pen and ink
*93*

**MY TEACHER'S HANDS**
Charcoal pencil
*99*

**THROUGH A GLASS DARKLY**
Pastel pencil
*104*

**HEAVEN . . . YOUR REAL HOME**
Pastel pencil
*106*

**ANCHORED BOAT IN SNOW**
Pen and ink
*112*

# SCRIPTURE ART BY JILL De HAAN

**1 CHRONICLES 16:11**

*6*

**EPHESIANS 2:10**

*13*

**ROMANS 12:12**

*24*

**PSALM 27:1**

*36*

**PHILIPPIANS 4:13**

*41*

# SCRIPTURE ART BY JILL De HAAN, CONTINUED

**ISAIAH 40:29**

*46*

**2 CORINTHIANS 12:9**

*63*

**JOHN 14:27**

*80*

**ROMANS 15:4**

*100*

**1 CORINTHIANS 2:9**

*113*

# *Beyond Suffering* Resources

## *Beyond Suffering®: A Christian View on Disability Ministry*

Study Guide by Joni Eareckson Tada and Steve Bundy with Pat Verbal

Leader's Guide by Joni Eareckson Tada and Kathy McReynolds, PhD

This groundbreaking course of study will transform the way Christians view God's plan for disability and suffering. The curriculum contains 16 lessons organized into four modules:

- Overview of Disability Ministry
- Theology of Suffering and Disability
- The Church and Disability Ministry
- Introduction to Bioethics

### *Beyond Suffering* Study Guide
291 pages with CD-ROM
**ISBN 978-0-9838484-0-0**

### *Beyond Suffering* Leader's Guide
1 CD-ROM, 2 DVDs
**ISBN 978-0-9838484-1-7**

Each module is designed to give Christians a solid understanding of the main issues involved in various aspects of disability ministry. Students who embrace this study will gain a sense of confidence in knowing they are part of a movement that God is orchestrating to fulfill his command in Luke 14:21: "Go quickly into the streets and alleys of the town and invite the poor, the crippled, the blind, and the lame."

## Also Available in Braille, Spanish, and iBooks Editions

### *Beyond Suffering* Braille Edition
Study Guide, Course Reader & Leader's Manual in a .brf format for use with Braille reading software and printers.
**ISBN 978-0-9838484-4-8**

### *Beyond Suffering* iBooks Edition
The downloadable, fully interactive version of the Study Guide and Leader's Guide for use on iPad comes alive with additional photos, videos, and graphics to inspire the 21st-century student. Available on iTunes.
**ISBN 978-0-9838484-5-5**

### *Beyond Suffering* Bible
The *Beyond Suffering Bible* is the first Bible to directly address those who suffer and the people who love and care for them.

Hardcover: **ISBN 978-1-4143-9202-8**

Softcover: **ISBN 978-1-4143-9558-6**

Teal/Brown/Rose Gold: **ISBN 978-1-4143-9561-6**

Brown/Tan: **ISBN 978-1-4143-9559-3**

Teal/Brown/Rose Gold indexed: **ISBN 978-1-4143-9562-3**

Brown/Tan indexed: **ISBN 978-1-4143-9560-9**

**www.joniandfriends.org**
P.O. Box 3333, Agoura Hills, CA 91376
818-707-5664 • TTY:818-707-9707

Christian Institute on Disability

CP1389